RESUMES FOR
FIRST-TIME JOB HUNTERS

THIRD EDITION

RESUMES FOR

FIRST-TIME

JOB HUNTERS

With Sample Cover Letters

The Editors of McGraw-Hill

McGraw-Hill

New York   Chicago   San Francisco   Lisbon   London   Madrid   Mexico City
Milan   New Delhi   San Juan   Seoul   Singapore   Sydney   Toronto

Library of Congress Cataloging-in-Publication Data

Resumes for first-time job hunters : with sample cover letters / the editors of McGraw-Hill
career books.—3rd ed.
      p.   cm. — (McGraw-Hill professional resumes series)
   ISBN 0-07-143852-1 (pbk. : alk. paper)
   1. Resumes (Employment)   I. Series.

  HF5383.R4376   2005
  650.14′2—dc22   2004059297

4 5 6 7 8 9 0 QSR QSR 0 9 8 7 6

ISBN 0-07-143852-1

McGraw-Hill books are available at special quantity discounts to use as premiums and sales
promotions, or for use in corporate training programs. For more information, please write to
the Director of Special Sales, Professional Publishing, McGraw-Hill, Two Penn Plaza, New
York, NY 10121-2298. Or contact your local bookstore.

This book is printed on acid-free paper.

Contents

Introduction

Your resume is a piece of paper (or an electronic document) that serves to introduce you to the people who will eventually hire you. To write a thoughtful resume, you must thoroughly assess your personality, your accomplishments, and the skills you have acquired. The act of composing and submitting a resume also requires you to carefully consider the company or individual that might hire you. What are they looking for, and how can you meet their needs? This book shows you how to organize your personal information and experience into a concise and well-written resume so that your qualifications and potential as an employee will be understood easily and quickly by a complete stranger.

Writing the resume is just one step in what can be a daunting job-search process, but it is an important element in the chain of events that will lead you to your new position. While you are probably a talented, bright, and charming person, your resume may not reflect these qualities. A poorly written resume can get you nowhere; a well-written resume can land you an interview and potentially a job. A good resume can even lead the interviewer to ask you questions that will allow you to talk about your strengths and highlight the skills you can bring to a prospective employer. Even a person with very little experience can find a good job if he or she is assisted by a thoughtful and polished resume.

Lengthy, typewritten resumes are a thing of the past. Today, employers do not have the time or the patience for verbose documents; they look for tightly composed, straightforward, action-based resumes. Although a one-page resume is the norm, a two-page resume may be warranted if you have had extensive job experience or have changed careers and truly need the space to properly position yourself. If, after careful editing, you still need more than one page to present yourself, it's acceptable to use a second page. A crowded resume that's hard to read would be the worst of your choices.

Distilling your work experience, education, and interests into such a small space requires preparation and thought. This book takes you step-by-step through the process of crafting an effective resume that will stand out in today's competitive marketplace. It serves as a workbook and a place to write down your experiences, while also including the techniques you'll need to pull all the necessary elements together. In the following pages, you'll find many examples of resumes that are specific to your area of interest. Study them for inspiration and find what appeals to you. There are a variety of ways to organize and present your information; inside, you'll find several that will be suitable to your needs. Good luck landing the job of your dreams!

The Elements of an Effective Resume

An effective resume is composed of information that employers are most interested in knowing about a prospective job applicant. This information is conveyed by a few essential elements. The following is a list of elements that are found in most resumes—some essential, some optional. Later in this chapter, we will further examine the role of each of these elements in the makeup of your resume.

- Heading
- Objective and/or Keyword Section
- Work Experience
- Education
- Honors
- Activities
- Certificates and Licenses
- Publications
- Professional Memberships
- Special Skills
- Personal Information
- References

The first step in preparing your resume is to gather information about yourself and your past accomplishments. Later you will refine this information, rewrite it using effective language, and organize it into an attractive layout. But first, let's take a look at each of these important elements individually so you can judge their appropriateness for your resume.

Heading

Although the heading may seem to be the simplest section of your resume, be careful not to take it lightly. It is the first section your prospective employer will see, and it contains the information she or he will need to contact you. At the very least, the heading must contain your name, your home address, and, of course, a phone number where you can be reached easily.

In today's high-tech world, many of us have multiple ways that we can be contacted. You may list your e-mail address if you are reasonably sure the employer makes use of this form of communication. Keep in mind, however, that others may have access to your e-mail messages if you send them from an account provided by your current company. If this is a concern, do not list your work e-mail address on your resume. If you are able to take calls at your current place of business, you should include your work number, because most employers will attempt to contact you during typical business hours.

If you have voice mail or a reliable answering machine at home or at work, list its number in the heading and make sure your greeting is professional and clear. Always include at least one phone number in your heading, even if it is a temporary number, where a prospective employer can leave a message.

You might have a dozen different ways to be contacted, but you do not need to list all of them. Confine your numbers or addresses to those that are the easiest for the prospective employer to use and the simplest for you to retrieve.

Objective

When seeking a specific career path, it is important to list a job or career objective on your resume. This statement helps employers know the direction you see yourself taking, so they can determine whether your goals are in line with those of their organization and the position available. Normally, an objective is one to two sentences long. Its contents will vary depending on your career field, goals, and personality. The objective can be specific or general, but it should always be to the point. See the sample resumes in this book for examples.

If you are planning to use this resume online, or you suspect your potential employer is likely to scan your resume, you will want to include a "keyword" in the objective. This allows a prospective employer, searching hundreds of resumes for a specific skill or position objective, to locate the keyword and find your resume. In essence, a keyword is what's "hot" in your particular field at a given time. It's a buzzword, a shorthand way of getting a particular message across at a glance. For example, if you are a lawyer, your objective might state your desire to work in the area of corporate litigation. In this case, someone searching for the keyword "corporate litigation" will pull up your resume and know that you want to plan, research, and present cases at trial on behalf of the corporation. If your objective states that you "desire a challenging position in systems design," the keyword is "systems design," an industry-specific shorthand way of saying that you want to be involved in assessing the need for, acquiring, and implementing high-technology systems. These are keywords and every industry has them, so it's becoming more and more important to include a few in your resume. (You may need to conduct additional research to make sure you know what keywords are most likely to be used in your desired industry, profession, or situation.)

There are many resume and job-search sites online. Like most things in the online world, they vary a great deal in quality. Use your discretion. If you plan to apply for jobs online or advertise your availability this way, you will want to design a scannable resume. This type of resume uses a format that can be easily scanned into a computer and added to a database. Scanning allows a prospective employer to use keywords to quickly review each applicant's experience and skills, and (in the event that there are many candidates for the job) to keep your resume for future reference.

Many people find that it is worthwhile to create two or more versions of their basic resume. You may want an intricately designed resume on high-quality paper to mail or hand out *and* a resume that is designed to be scanned into a computer and saved on a database or an online job site. You can even create a resume in ASCII text to e-mail to prospective employers. For further information, you may wish to refer to the *Guide to Internet Job Searching*, by Frances Roehm and Margaret Dikel, updated and published every other year by McGraw-Hill. This excellent book contains helpful and detailed information about formatting a resume for Internet use. To get you started, in Chapter 3 we have included a list of things to keep in mind when creating electronic resumes.

Although it is usually a good idea to include an objective, in some cases this element is not necessary. The goal of the objective statement is to provide the employer with an idea of where you see yourself going in the field. However, if you are uncertain of the exact nature of the job you seek, including an objective that is too specific could result in your not being considered for a host of perfectly acceptable positions. If you decide not to use an objective heading in your resume, you should definitely incorporate the information that would be conveyed in the objective into your cover letter.

Work Experience

Work experience is arguably the most important element of them all. Unless you are a recent graduate or former homemaker with little or no relevant work experience, your current and former positions will provide the central focus of the resume. You will want this section to be as complete and carefully constructed as possible. By thoroughly examining your work experience, you can get to the heart of your accomplishments and present them in a way that demonstrates and highlights your qualifications.

If you are just entering the workforce, your resume will probably focus on your education, but you should also include information on your work or volunteer experiences. Although you will have less information about work experience than a person who has held multiple positions or is advanced in his or her career, the amount of information is not what is most important in this section. How the information is presented and what it says about you as a worker and a person are what really count.

As you create this section of your resume, remember the need for accuracy. Include all the necessary information about each of your jobs, including your job title, dates of employment, name of your employer, city, state, responsibilities, special projects you handled, and accomplishments. Be sure to list only accomplishments for which you were directly responsible. And don't be alarmed if you haven't participated in or worked on special projects, because this section may not be relevant to certain jobs.

The most common way to list your work experience is in *reverse chronological order*. In other words, start with your most recent job and work your way backward. This way, your prospective employer sees your current (and often most important) position before considering your past employment. Your most recent position, if it's the most important in terms of responsibilities and relevance to the job for which you are applying, should also be the one that includes the most information as compared to your previous positions.

Even if the work itself seems unrelated to your proposed career path, you should list any job or experience that will help sell your talents. If you were promoted or given greater responsibilities or commendations, be sure to mention the fact.

The following worksheet is provided to help you organize your experiences in the working world. It will also serve as an excellent resource to refer to when updating your resume in the future.

WORK EXPERIENCE

Job One:

Job Title _____

Dates _____

Employer _____

City, State _____

Major Duties _____

_____

_____

_____

_____

_____

_____

_____

_____

Special Projects _____

_____

_____

_____

Accomplishments _____

_____

_____

_____

_____

_____

Job Two:

Job Title _____

Dates _____

Employer _____

City, State _____

Major Duties _____

_____

_____

_____

_____

_____

_____

_____

Special Projects _____

_____

_____

_____

Accomplishments _____

_____

_____

_____

_____

_____

_____

_____

_____

Job Three:

Job Title _____

Dates _____

Employer _____

City, State _____

Major Duties _____

_____

_____

_____

_____

_____

_____

_____

Special Projects _____

_____

_____

Accomplishments _____

_____

_____

_____

_____

_____

_____

_____

Job Four:

Job Title _____

Dates _____

Employer _____

City, State _____

Major Duties _____

_____

_____

_____

_____

_____

_____

_____

Special Projects _____

_____

_____

_____

Accomplishments _____

_____

_____

_____

_____

_____

_____

_____

Education

Education is usually the second most important element of a resume. Your educational background is often a deciding factor in an employer's decision to interview you. Highlight your accomplishments in school as much as you did those accomplishments at work. If you are looking for your first professional job, your education or life experience will be your greatest asset because your related work experience will be minimal. In this case, the education section becomes the most important means of selling yourself.

Include in this section all the degrees or certificates you have received; your major or area of concentration; all of the honors you earned; and any relevant activities you participated in, organized, or chaired. Again, list your most recent schooling first. If you have completed graduate-level work, begin with that and work your way back through your undergraduate education. If you have completed college, you generally should not list your high-school experience; do so only if you earned special honors, you had a grade point average that was much better than the norm, or this was your highest level of education.

If you have completed a large number of credit hours in a subject that may be relevant to the position you are seeking but did not obtain a degree, you may wish to list the hours or classes you completed. Keep in mind, however, that you may be asked to explain why you did not finish the program. If you are currently in school, list the degree, certificate, or license you expect to obtain and the projected date of completion.

The following worksheet will help you gather the information you need for this section of your resume.

EDUCATION

School One _____

Major or Area of Concentration _____

Degree _____

Dates _____

School Two _____

Major or Area of Concentration _____

Degree _____

Dates _____

Honors

If you include an honors section in your resume, you should highlight any awards, honors, or memberships in honorary societies that you have received. (You may also incorporate this information into your education section.) Often, the honors are academic in nature, but this section also may be used for special achievements in sports, clubs, or other school activities. Always include the name of the organization awarding the honor and the date(s) received. Use the following worksheet to help you gather your information.

HONORS

Honor One _____

Awarding Organization _____

Date(s) _____

Honor Two _____

Awarding Organization _____

Date(s) _____

Honor Three _____

Awarding Organization _____

Date(s) _____

Honor Four _____

Awarding Organization _____

Date(s) _____

Honor Five _____

Awarding Organization _____

Date(s) _____

Activities

Perhaps you have been active in different organizations or clubs; often an employer will look at such involvement as evidence of initiative, dedication, and good social skills. Examples of your ability to take a leading role in a group should be included on a resume, if you can provide them. The activities section of your resume should present neighborhood and community activities, volunteer positions, and so forth. In general, you may want to avoid listing any organization whose name indicates the race, creed, sex, age, marital status, sexual orientation, or nation of origin of its members because this could expose you to discrimination. Use the following worksheet to list the specifics of your activities.

ACTIVITIES

Organization/Activity _____

Accomplishments _____

_____

_____

Organization/Activity _____

Accomplishments _____

_____

_____

Organization/Activity _____

Accomplishments _____

_____

_____

As your work experience grows through the years, your school activities and honors will carry less weight and be emphasized less in your resume. Eventually, you will probably list only your degree and any major honors received. As time goes by, your job performance and the experience you've gained become the most important elements in your resume, which should change to reflect this.

Certificates and Licenses

If your chosen career path requires specialized training, you may already have certificates or licenses. You should list these if the job you are seeking requires them and you, of course, have acquired them. If you have applied for a license but have not yet received it, use the phrase "application pending."

License requirements vary by state. If you have moved or are planning to relocate to another state, check with that state's board or licensing agency for all licensing requirements.

Always make sure that all of the information you list is completely accurate. Locate copies of your certificates and licenses, and check the exact date and name of the accrediting agency. Use the following worksheet to organize the necessary information.

CERTIFICATES AND LICENSES

Name of License _____

Licensing Agency _____

Date Issued _____

Name of License _____

Licensing Agency _____

Date Issued _____

Name of License _____

Licensing Agency _____

Date Issued _____

Publications

Some professions strongly encourage or even require that you publish. If you have written, coauthored, or edited any books, articles, professional papers, or works of a similar nature that pertain to your field, you will definitely want to include this element. Remember to list the date of publication and the publisher's name, and specify whether you were the sole author or a coauthor. Book, magazine, or journal titles are generally italicized, while the titles of articles within a larger publication appear in quotes. (Check with your reference librarian for more about the appropriate way to present this information.) For scientific or research papers, you will need to give the date, place, and audience to whom the paper was presented.

Use the following worksheet to help you gather the necessary information about your publications.

PUBLICATIONS

Title and Type (Note, Article, etc.) _____

Title of Publication (Journal, Book, etc.) _____

Publisher _____

Date Published _____

Title and Type (Note, Article, etc.) _____

Title of Publication (Journal, Book, etc.) _____

Publisher _____

Date Published _____

Title and Type (Note, Article, etc.) _____

Title of Publication (Journal, Book, etc.) _____

Publisher _____

Date Published _____

Professional Memberships

Another potential element in your resume is a section listing professional memberships. Use this section to describe your involvement in professional associations, unions, and similar organizations. It is to your advantage to list any professional memberships that pertain to the job you are seeking. Many employers see your membership as representative of your desire to stay up-to-date and connected in your field. Include the dates of your involvement and whether you took part in any special activities or held any offices within the organization. Use the following worksheet to organize your information.

PROFESSIONAL MEMBERSHIPS

Name of Organization _____

Office(s) Held_____

Activities _____

Dates _____

Name of Organization _____

Office(s) Held_____

Activities _____

Dates _____

Name of Organization _____

Office(s) Held_____

Activities _____

Dates _____

Name of Organization _____

Office(s) Held_____

Activities _____

Dates _____

Special Skills

The special skills section of your resume is the place to mention any special abilities you have that relate to the job you are seeking. You can use this element to present certain talents or experiences that are not necessarily a part of your education or work experience. Common examples include fluency in a foreign language, extensive travel abroad, or knowledge of a particular computer application. "Special skills" can encompass a wide range of talents, and this section can be used creatively. However, for each skill you list, you should be able to describe how it would be a direct asset in the type of work you're seeking because employers may ask just that in an interview. If you can't think of a way to do this, it may be extraneous information.

Personal Information

Some people include personal information on their resumes. This is generally not recommended, but you might wish to include it if you think that something in your personal life, such as a hobby or talent, has some bearing on the position you are seeking. This type of information is often referred to at the beginning of an interview, when it may be used as an icebreaker. Of course, personal information regarding your age, marital status, race, religion, or sexual orientation should never appear on your resume as personal information. It should be given only in the context of memberships and activities, and only when doing so would not expose you to discrimination.

References

References are not usually given on the resume itself, but a prospective employer needs to know that you have references who may be contacted if necessary. All you need to include is a single sentence at the end of the resume: "References are available upon request," or even simply, "References available." Have a reference list ready—your interviewer may ask to see it! Contact each person on the list ahead of time to see whether it is all right for you to use him or her as a reference. This way, the person has a chance to think about what to say *before* the call occurs. This helps ensure that you will obtain the best reference possible.

Chapter 2

Writing Your Resume

Now that you have gathered the information for each section of your resume, it's time to write it out in a way that will get the attention of the reviewer—hopefully, your future employer! The language you use in your resume will affect its success, so you must be careful and conscientious. Translate the facts you have gathered into the active, precise language of resume writing. You will be aiming for a resume that keeps the reader's interest and highlights your accomplishments in a concise and effective way.

Resume writing is unlike any other form of writing. Although your seventh-grade composition teacher would not approve, the rules of punctuation and sentence building are often completely ignored. Instead, you should try for a functional, direct writing style that focuses on the use of verbs and other words that imply action on your part. Writing with action words and strong verbs characterizes you to potential employers as an energetic, active person, someone who completes tasks and achieves results from his or her work. Resumes that do not make use of action words can sound passive and stale. These resumes are not effective and do not get the attention of any employer, no matter how qualified the applicant. Choose words that display your strengths and demonstrate your initiative. The following list of commonly used verbs will help you create a strong resume:

administered	assembled
advised	assumed responsibility
analyzed	billed
arranged	built

carried out	inspected
channeled	interviewed
collected	introduced
communicated	invented
compiled	maintained
completed	managed
conducted	met with
contacted	motivated
contracted	negotiated
coordinated	operated
counseled	orchestrated
created	ordered
cut	organized
designed	oversaw
determined	performed
developed	planned
directed	prepared
dispatched	presented
distributed	produced
documented	programmed
edited	published
established	purchased
expanded	recommended
functioned as	recorded
gathered	reduced
handled	referred
hired	represented
implemented	researched
improved	reviewed

saved	supervised
screened	taught
served as	tested
served on	trained
sold	typed
suggested	wrote

Let's look at two examples that differ only in their writing style. The first resume section is ineffective because it does not use action words to accent the applicant's work experiences.

WORK EXPERIENCE
Regional Sales Manager

Manager of sales representatives from seven states. Manager of twelve food chain accounts in the East. In charge of the sales force's planned selling toward specific goals. Supervisor and trainer of new sales representatives. Consulting for customers in the areas of inventory management and quality control.

Special Projects: Coordinator and sponsor of annual Food Industry Seminar.

Accomplishments: Monthly regional volume went up 25 percent during my tenure while, at the same time, a proper sales/cost ratio was maintained. Customer-company relations were improved.

In the following paragraph, we have rewritten the same section using action words. Notice how the tone has changed. It now sounds stronger and more active. This person accomplished goals and really *did* things.

WORK EXPERIENCE
Regional Sales Manager

Managed sales representatives from seven states. Oversaw twelve food chain accounts in the eastern United States. Directed the sales force in planned selling toward specific goals. Supervised and trained new sales representatives. Counseled customers in the areas of inventory management and quality control. Coordinated and sponsored the annual Food Industry Seminar. Increased monthly regional volume by 25 percent and helped to improve customer-company relations during my tenure.

One helpful way to construct the work experience section is to make use of your actual job descriptions—the written duties and expectations your employers have for a person in your current or former position. Job descriptions are rarely written in proper resume language, so you will have to rework them, but they do include much of the information necessary to create this section of your resume. If you have access to job descriptions for your former positions, you can use the details to construct an action-oriented paragraph. Often, your human resources department can provide a job description for your current position.

The following is an example of a typical human resources job description, followed by a rewritten version of the same description employing action words and specific details about the job. Again, pay attention to the style of writing instead of the content, as the details of your own experience will be unique.

WORK EXPERIENCE
Public Administrator I

Responsibilities: Coordinate and direct public services to meet the needs of the nation, state, or community. Analyze problems; work with special committees and public agencies; recommend solutions to governing bodies.

Aptitudes and Skills: Ability to relate to and communicate with people; solve complex problems through analysis; plan, organize, and implement policies and programs. Knowledge of political systems, financial management, personnel administration, program evaluation, and organizational theory.

WORK EXPERIENCE
Public Administrator I

Wrote pamphlets and conducted discussion groups to inform citizens of legislative processes and consumer issues. Organized and supervised 25 interviewers. Trained interviewers in effective communication skills.

After you have written out your resume, you are ready to begin the next important step: assembly and layout.

Chapter 3

Assembly and Layout

At this point, you've gathered all the necessary information for your resume and rewritten it in language that will impress your potential employers. Your next step is to assemble the sections in a logical order and lay them out on the page neatly and attractively to achieve the desired effect: getting the interview.

Assembly

The order of the elements in a resume makes a difference in its overall effect. Clearly, you would not want to bury your name and address somewhere in the middle of the resume. Nor would you want to lead with a less important section, such as special skills. Put the elements in an order that stresses your most important accomplishments and the things that will be most appealing to your potential employer. For example, if you are new to the workforce, you will want the reviewer to read about your education and life skills before any part-time jobs you may have held for short durations. On the other hand, if you have been gainfully employed for several years and currently hold an important position in your company, you should list your work accomplishments ahead of your educational information, which has become less pertinent with time.

Certain things should always be included in your resume, but others are optional. The following list shows you which are which. You might want to use it as a checklist to be certain that you have included all of the necessary information.

Essential	**Optional**
Name	Cellular Phone Number
Address	Pager Number
Phone Number	E-Mail Address or Website Address
Work Experience	Voice Mail Number
Education	Job Objective
References Phrase	Honors
	Special Skills
	Publications
	Professional Memberships
	Activities
	Certificates and Licenses
	Personal Information
	Graphics
	Photograph

Your choice of optional sections depends on your own background and employment needs. Always use information that will put you in a favorable light—unless it's absolutely essential, avoid anything that will prompt the interviewer to ask questions about your weaknesses or something else that could be unflattering. Make sure your information is accurate and truthful. If your honors are impressive, include them in the resume. If your activities in school demonstrate talents that are necessary for the job you are seeking, allow space for a section on activities. If you are applying for a position that requires ornamental illustration, you may want to include border illustrations or graphics that demonstrate your talents in this area. If you are answering an advertisement for a job that requires certain physical traits, a photo of yourself might be appropriate. A person applying for a job as a computer programmer would *not* include a photo as part of his or her resume. Each resume is unique, just as each person is unique.

Types of Resumes

So far we have focused on the most common type of resume—the *reverse chronological* resume—in which your most recent job is listed first. This is the type of resume usually preferred by those who have to read a large number of resumes, and it is by far the most popular and widely circulated. However, this style of presentation may not be the most effective way to highlight *your* skills and accomplishments.

For example, if you are reentering the workforce after many years or are trying to change career fields, the *functional* resume may work best. This type of resume puts the focus on your achievements instead of the sequence of your work history. In the functional resume, your experience is presented through your general accomplishments and the skills you have developed in your working life.

A functional resume is assembled from the same information you gathered in Chapter 1. The main difference lies in how you organize the information. Essentially, the work experience section is divided in two, with your job duties and accomplishments constituting one section and your employers' names, cities, and states; your positions; and the dates employed making up the other. Place the first section near the top of your resume, just below your job objective (if used), and call it *Accomplishments* or *Achievements*. The second section, containing the bare essentials of your work history, should come after the accomplishments section and can be called *Employment History*, since it is a chronological overview of your former jobs.

The other sections of your resume remain the same. The work experience section is the only one affected in the functional format. By placing the section that focuses on your achievements at the beginning, you draw attention to these achievements. This puts less emphasis on where you worked and when, and more on what you did and what you are capable of doing.

If you are changing careers, the emphasis on skills and achievements is important. The identities of previous employers (who aren't part of your new career field) need to be downplayed. A functional resume can help accomplish this task. If you are reentering the workforce after a long absence, a functional resume is the obvious choice. And if you lack full-time work experience, you will need to draw attention away from this fact and put the focus on your skills and abilities. You may need to highlight your volunteer activities and part-time work. Education may also play a more important role in your resume.

The type of resume that is right for you will depend on your personal circumstances. It may be helpful to create both types and then compare them. Which one presents you in the best light? Examples of both types of resumes are included in this book. Use the sample resumes in Chapter 5 to help you decide on the content, presentation, and look of your own resume.

Resume or Curriculum Vitae?

A curriculum vitae (CV) is a longer, more detailed synopsis of your professional history, which generally runs three or more pages in length. It includes a summary of your educational and academic background as well as teaching and research experience, publications, presentations, awards, honors, affiliations, and other details. Because the purpose of the CV is different from that of the resume, many of the rules we've discussed thus far involving style and length do not apply.

A curriculum vitae is used primarily for admissions applications to graduate or professional schools, independent consulting in a variety of settings, proposals for fellowships or grants, or applications for positions in academia. As with a resume, you may need different versions of a CV for different types of positions. You should only send a CV when one is specifically requested by an employer or institution.

Like a resume, your CV should include your name, contact information, education, skills, and experience. In addition to the basics, a CV includes research and teaching experience, publications, grants and fellowships, professional associations and licenses, awards, and other information relevant to the position for which you are applying. You can follow the advice presented thus far to gather and organize your personal information.

Special Tips for Electronic Resumes

Because there are many details to consider in writing a resume that will be posted or transmitted on the Internet, or one that will be scanned into a computer when it is received, we suggest that you refer to the *Guide to Internet Job Searching*, by Frances Roehm and Margaret Dikel, as previously mentioned. However, here are some brief, general guidelines to follow if you expect your resume to be scanned into a computer.

- Use standard fonts in which none of the letters touch.

- Keep in mind that underlining, italics, and fancy scripts may not scan well.

- Use boldface and capitalization to set off elements. Again, make sure letters don't touch. Leave at least a quarter inch between lines of type.

- Keep information and elements at the left margin. Centering, columns, and even indenting may change when the resume is optically scanned.

- Do not use any lines, boxes, or graphics.

- Place the most important information at the top of the first page. If you use two pages, put "Page 1 of 2" at the bottom of the first page and put your name and "Page 2 of 2" at the top of the second page.

- List each telephone number on its own line in the header.

- Use multiple keywords or synonyms for what you do to make sure your qualifications will be picked up if a prospective employer is searching for them. Use nouns that are keywords for your profession.

- Be descriptive in your titles. For example, don't just use "assistant"; use "legal office assistant."

- Make sure the contrast between print and paper is good. Use a high-quality laser printer and white or very light colored 8½-by-11-inch paper.

- Mail a high-quality laser print or an excellent copy. Do not fold or use staples, as this might interfere with scanning. You may, however, use paper clips.

In addition to creating a resume that works well for scanning, you may want to have a resume that can be e-mailed to reviewers. Because you may not know what word processing application the recipient uses, the best format to use is ASCII text. (ASCII stands for "American Standard Code for Information Interchange.") It allows people with very different software platforms to exchange and understand information. (E-mail operates on this principle.) ASCII is a simple, text-only language, which means you can include only simple text. There can be no use of boldface, italics, or even paragraph indentations.

To create an ASCII resume, just use your normal word processing program; when finished, save it as a "text only" document. You will find this option under the "save" or "save as" command. Here is a list of things to *avoid* when crafting your electronic resume:

- Tabs. Use your space bar. Tabs will not work.

- Any special characters, such as mathematical symbols.

- Word wrap. Use hard returns (the return key) to make line breaks.

- Centering or other formatting. Align everything at the left margin.

- Bold or italic fonts. Everything will be converted to plain text when you save the file as a "text only" document.

Check carefully for any mistakes before you save the document as a text file. Spellcheck and proofread it several times; then ask someone with a keen eye to go over it again for you. Remember: the key is to keep it simple. Any attempt to make this resume pretty or decorative may result in a resume that is confusing and hard to read. After you have saved the document, you can cut and paste it into an e-mail or onto a website.

Layout for a Paper Resume

A great deal of care—and much more formatting—is necessary to achieve an attractive layout for your paper resume. There is no single appropriate layout that applies to every resume, but there are a few basic rules to follow in putting your resume on paper:

- Leave a comfortable margin on the sides, top, and bottom of the page (usually one to one and a half inches).

- Use appropriate spacing between the sections (two to three line spaces are usually adequate).

- Be consistent in the *type* of headings you use for different sections of your resume. For example, if you capitalize the heading EMPLOY-MENT HISTORY, don't use initial capitals and underlining for a section of equal importance, such as Education.

- Do not use more than one font in your resume. Stay consistent by choosing a font that is fairly standard and easy to read, and don't change it for different sections. Beware of the tendency to try to make your resume original by choosing fancy type styles; your resume may end up looking unprofessional instead of creative. Unless you are in a very creative and artistic field, you should almost always stick with tried-and-true type styles like Times New Roman and Palatino, which are often used in business writing. In the area of resume styles, conservative is usually the best way to go.

CHRONOLOGICAL RESUME

Jennifer Rosales

381 Ponderosa Avenue • Albuquerque, NM 87198
(505) 555-3578 • jennifer.rosales@xxx.com

GOAL

A position that utilizes my strong organizational and multitasking skills.

WORK EXPERIENCE

August 2004 to May 2005
Food Service Worker. Kentucky Fried Chicken, Albuquerque, NM.
Responsibilities: Taking and preparing food orders, running cash register, stocking supplies, and cleaning kitchen and eating areas.

May 2004 to August 2004
Receptionist. Santa Fe Real Estate Company, Albuquerque, NM.
Responsibilities: Answering phones and calling customers for further information pertaining to their homes. Maintaining client contacts via Microsoft Office Outlook.

Prior to May 2004
Babysitter.

OTHER EXPERIENCE

- I am a student in O.W.E., "Outside Work Experience," learning about jobs and future careers.
- I am fluent in Spanish.
- I was a volunteer camp counselor working with children aged 11 to 13, assisting with sports and recreational activities.
- I was a member of the following Albuquerque High School groups: Unity Among Us, Students in Christian Fellowship, Student Body Council, and Going Places Academically.
- I am involved with church activities.

EDUCATION

I am a graduate of Albuquerque High School, 2004.
My future educational plans are to attend Albuquerque Technical and Vocational Institute.

REFERENCES

Available upon request.

FUNCTIONAL RESUME

MICHAEL SUTHERLAND
2757 Dolphin Dr. • Arnold, MD 21012 • (301) 555-5390 • michael.sutherland@xxx.com

OBJECTIVE
A part-time position as an usher

EDUCATION
UCLA School of Theater, Film, and TV, beginning Fall 2004
Comprehensive Major: Directing and Theater Management

Arnold High School, June 2004
Forensics Competitive Speech Team (four years)
Drama and Musical Productions (three years)

AWARDS
- Bank of Maryland Fine Arts Award—2nd place, Region Finals Scholarship, 2004
- Veterans of Foreign Wars Speech Award, 2003 and 2004
- Student of the Year—Arnold High School, 2003
- Boys' State Delegate, 2003
- State Forensics for Thematic Interpretation, 21st place (Pieces included: *Torch Song Trilogy, Into the Woods, Brighton Beach Memoirs, Measure for Measure*), 2003
- Rotary Speech Award, 2001 and 2002
- Walter Johnson Musical Comedy Award at Anne Arundel Community Stage, 2001

PERFORMANCE THEATER EXPERIENCE
Director, Collaborator, and Performer, AIDS Teen Theater, 2004
"Billy Crocker" in *Anything Goes*, 2003
"Vincentio" in *Taming of the Shrew*, 2003
"Albert" in *Bye-Bye Birdie*, 2002
"Frank Butler" in *Annie Get Your Gun*, 2001
"Charlie" in *Charlie and the Chocolate Factory*, 2001

TECHNICAL AND MANAGING THEATER EXPERIENCE
Anne Arundel Community Stage
Production Assistant—*Fiddler on the Roof*, 2004
Assistant Stage Manager—*Into the Woods*, 2002
Assistant Stage Manager—*Camelot*, 2001
Chorus and Stagehand—*Evita*, 2000
Stagehand—*My Fair Lady*, 2000

REFERENCES
Available upon request

- Always try to fit your resume on one page. If you are having trouble with this, you may be trying to say too much. Edit out any repetitive or unnecessary information, and shorten descriptions of earlier jobs where possible. Ask a friend you trust for feedback on what seems unnecessary or unimportant. For example, you may have included too many optional sections. Today, with the prevalence of the personal computer as a tool, there is no excuse for a poorly laid out resume. Experiment with variations until you are pleased with the result.

Remember that a resume is not an autobiography. Too much information will only get in the way. The more compact your resume, the easier it will be to review. If a person who is swamped with resumes looks at yours, catches the main points, and then calls you for an interview to fill in some of the details, your resume has already accomplished its task. A clear and concise resume makes for a happy reader and a good impression.

There are times when, despite extensive editing, the resume simply cannot fit on one page. In this case, the resume should be laid out on two pages in such a way that neither clarity nor appearance is compromised. Each page of a two-page resume should be marked clearly: the first should indicate "Page 1 of 2," and the second should include your name and the page number, for example, "Julia Ramirez—Page 2 of 2." The pages should then be paper-clipped together. You may use a smaller type size (in the same font as the body of your resume) for the page numbers. Place them at the bottom of page one and the top of page two. Again, spend the time now to experiment with the layout until you find one that looks good to you.

Always show your final layout to other people and ask them what they like or dislike about it, and what impresses them most when they read your resume. Make sure that their responses are the same as what you want to elicit from your prospective employer. If they aren't the same, you should continue to make changes until the necessary information is emphasized.

Proofreading

After you have finished typing the master copy of your resume and before you have it copied or printed, thoroughly check it for typing and spelling errors. Do not place all your trust in your computer's spellcheck function. Use an old editing trick and read the whole resume backward—start at the end and read it right to left and bottom to top. This can help you see the small errors or inconsistencies that are easy to overlook. Take time to do it right because a single error on a document this important can cause the reader to judge your attention to detail in a harsh light.

Have several people look at the finished resume just in case you've missed an error. Don't try to take a shortcut; not having an unbiased set of eyes examine your resume now could mean embarrassment later. Even experienced editors can easily overlook their own errors. Be thorough and conscientious with your proofreading so your first impression is a perfect one.

We have included the following rules of capitalization and punctuation to assist you in the final stage of creating your resume. Remember that resumes often require use of a shorthand style of writing that may include sentences without periods and other stylistic choices that break the standard rules of grammar. Be consistent in each section and throughout the whole resume with your choices.

RULES OF CAPITALIZATION

- Capitalize proper nouns, such as names of schools, colleges, and universities; names of companies; and brand names of products.

- Capitalize major words in the names and titles of books, tests, and articles that appear in the body of your resume.

- Capitalize words in major section headings of your resume.

- Do not capitalize words just because they seem important.

- When in doubt, consult a style manual such as *Words into Type* (Prentice Hall) or *The Chicago Manual of Style* (The University of Chicago Press). Your local library can help you locate these and other reference books. Many computer programs also have grammar help sections.

RULES OF PUNCTUATION

- Use commas to separate words in a series.

- Use a semicolon to separate series of words that already include commas within the series. (For an example, see the first rule of capitalization.)

- Use a semicolon to separate independent clauses that are not joined by a conjunction.

- Use a period to end a sentence.

- Use a colon to show that examples or details follow that will expand or amplify the preceding phrase.

- Avoid the use of dashes.

- Avoid the use of brackets.

- If you use any punctuation in an unusual way in your resume, be consistent in its use.

- Whenever you are uncertain, consult a style manual.

Putting Your Resume in Print

You will need to buy high-quality paper for your printer before you print your finished resume. Regular office paper is not good enough for resumes; the reviewer will probably think it looks flimsy and cheap. Go to an office supply store or copy shop and select a high-quality bond paper that will make a good first impression. Select colors like white, off-white, or possibly a light gray. In some industries, a pastel may be acceptable, but be sure the color and feel of the paper make a subtle, positive statement about you. Nothing in the choice of paper should be loud or unprofessional.

If your computer printer does not reproduce your resume properly and produces smudged or stuttered type, either ask to borrow a friend's or take your disk (or a clean original) to a printer or copy shop for high-quality copying. If you anticipate needing a large number of copies, taking your resume to a copy shop or a printer is probably the best choice.

Hold a sheet of your unprinted bond paper up to the light. If it has a watermark, you will want to point this out to the person helping you with copies; the printing should be done so that the reader can read the print and see the watermark the right way up. Check each copy for smudges or streaks. This is the time to be a perfectionist—the results of your careful preparation will be well worth it.

Chapter 4

The Cover Letter

Once your resume has been assembled, laid out, and printed to your satisfaction, the next and final step before distribution is to write your cover letter. Though there may be instances where you deliver your resume in person, you will usually send it through the mail or online. Resumes sent through the mail always need an accompanying letter that briefly introduces you and your resume. The purpose of the cover letter is to get a potential employer to read your resume, just as the purpose of the resume is to get that same potential employer to call you for an interview.

Like your resume, your cover letter should be clean, neat, and direct. A cover letter usually includes the following information:

1. Your name and address (unless it already appears on your personal letterhead) and your phone number(s); see item 7.

2. The date.

3. The name and address of the person and company to whom you are sending your resume.

4. The salutation ("Dear Mr." or "Dear Ms." followed by the person's last name, or "To Whom It May Concern" if you are answering a blind ad).

5. An opening paragraph explaining why you are writing (for example, in response to an ad, as a follow-up to a previous meeting, at the suggestion of someone you both know) and indicating that you are interested in whatever job is being offered.

6. One or more paragraphs that tell why you want to work for the company and what qualifications and experiences you can bring to the position. This is a good place to mention some detail about

that particular company that makes you want to work for them; this shows that you have done some research before applying.

7. A final paragraph that closes the letter and invites the reviewer to contact you for an interview. This can be a good place to tell the potential employer which method would be best to use when contacting you. Be sure to give the correct phone number and a good time to reach you, if that is important. You may mention here that your references are available upon request.

8. The closing ("Sincerely" or "Yours truly") followed by your signature in a dark ink, with your name typed under it.

Your cover letter should include all of this information and be no longer than one page in length. The language used should be polite, businesslike, and to the point. Don't attempt to tell your life story in the cover letter; a long and cluttered letter will serve only to annoy the reader. Remember that you need to mention only a few of your accomplishments and skills in the cover letter. The rest of your information is available in your resume. If your cover letter is a success, your resume will be read and all pertinent information reviewed by your prospective employer.

Producing the Cover Letter

Cover letters should always be individualized because they are always written to specific individuals and companies. Never use a form letter for your cover letter or copy it as you would a resume. Each cover letter should be unique, and as personal and lively as possible. (Of course, once you have written and rewritten your first cover letter until you are satisfied with it, you can certainly use similar wording in subsequent letters. You may want to save a template on your computer for future reference.) Keep a hard copy of each cover letter so you know exactly what you wrote in each one.

There are sample cover letters in Chapter 6. Use them as models or for ideas of how to assemble and lay out your own cover letters. Remember that every letter is unique and depends on the particular circumstances of the individual writing it and the job for which he or she is applying.

After you have written your cover letter, proofread it as thoroughly as you did your resume. Again, spelling or punctuation errors are a sure sign of carelessness, and you don't want that to be a part of your first impression on a prospective employer. This is no time to trust your spellcheck function. Even after going through a spelling and grammar check, your cover letter should be carefully proofread by at least one other person.

Print the cover letter on the same quality bond paper you used for your resume. Remember to sign it, using a good dark-ink pen. Handle the letter and resume carefully to avoid smudging or wrinkling, and mail them together in an appropriately sized envelope. Many stores sell matching envelopes to coordinate with your choice of bond paper.

Keep an accurate record of all resumes you send out and the results of each mailing. This record can be kept on your computer, in a calendar or notebook, or on file cards. Knowing when a resume is likely to have been received will keep you on track as you make follow-up phone calls.

About a week after mailing resumes and cover letters to potential employers, contact them by telephone. Confirm that your resume arrived and ask whether an interview might be possible. Be sure to record the name of the person you spoke to and any other information you gleaned from the conversation. It is wise to treat the person answering the phone with a great deal of respect; sometimes the assistant or receptionist has the ear of the person doing the hiring.

You should make a great impression with the strong, straightforward resume and personalized cover letter you have just created. We wish you every success in securing the career of your dreams!

Chapter 5

Sample Resumes

This chapter contains dozens of sample resumes for people pursuing a wide variety of jobs and careers.

There are many different styles of resumes in terms of graphic layout and presentation of information. These samples represent people with varying amounts of education and experience. Use them as models for your own resume. Choose one resume or borrow elements from several different resumes to help you design your own.

Timothy J. Comer

3825 West Thunderbird Way • Three Lakes, WI 54562 • (715) 555-1878
Timothy.Comer@xxx.com

Objective
Summer employment in which I can work and serve people. Salaried position preferred.

Education
Three Lakes High School, 2000–2004
General education / Honors and Advanced Placement courses

Experience
2002–2004
Snowy Sam's Restaurant, Eagle River, WI; Sales and Cleaning.
Responsibilities included opening, serving customers, keeping track of money, balancing the money at the end of the day, and securing the building.

Capabilities
Excellent organizational skills
Responsible
Proficient in the use of cash registers and Macintosh computers
Able to work with people
Skilled in working independently

Achievements
2003–2004
Commissioner of Homecoming and Elections, Associated Student Body; Principal's Highest Honor Roll
2002–2003
Class Treasurer; Principal's Honor Roll
2001–2002
Commissioner of Desegregation, Associated Student Body; Principal's Honor Roll
2000–2001
House of Representatives Alternate; Principal's Honor Roll

Affiliations
Three Lakes Football Team
Three Lakes Track-and-Field Team

Awards
Outstanding Leadership Award, Class of 2004
Three Lakes Football Scout Team Player of the Year, 2003

References
Available upon request

JONATHAN DEAN COURIER

8638 Walter Drive
Evanston, IL 60204
(847) 555-4825
jonathan.courier@xxx.net

CAREER OBJECTIVE

An engineering position involving civil/structural analysis and design

EDUCATION

Northwestern University
Master of Science degree in Civil Engineering
Credits completed toward degree: 21/33

Bachelor of Science degree in Civil Engineering, 2004
Major: Structural Engineering
Minors: Geotechnical Engineering and Construction

Engineer-in-Training, Illinois

WORK EXPERIENCE

Summer 2005   Elijah's Architects & Engineers, Inc., Chicago, IL
                 Engineering Intern
                 Worked in the structural division, dealing with the design
                 of criminal justice and educational facilities.

2004–2005   School of Civil Engineering, Northwestern University,
                 Evanston, IL
                 Teaching Assistant
                 Helped with Architectural Engineering, Structural Steel
                 Design, and Senior Design classes; tasks included instruc-
                 tion and grading of students.

Summer 2004   Civil Engineering Buildings, Northwestern University,
                 Evanston, IL
                 Building Receiving Technician
                 Handled various assignments during the final construction
                 phases of new additions.

ACTIVITIES AND HONORS

Distinguished Student, Fall 2003
Student Member, American Society of Civil Engineers
Theta Chi Honorary: Marshal, Spring 2003, and President, Fall 2004

References available upon request.

MIGUEL ROSAS
mrosas@xxx.com

Campus Address
434 J. Pierce Hall
Arizona State University
Tempe, AZ 85287
(602) 555-1328

Permanent Address
836 High Street
Reno, NV 89512
(702) 555-7206

OBJECTIVE
To obtain a position as an engineer in the field of Civil Engineering.

EDUCATION
Arizona State University, 2004
B.S., Civil Engineering, with a Structural Engineering emphasis.

EXPERIENCE
PRIORITY COURIER, Reno, NV
Courier
* Picked up and delivered bank bags.
* Handled special delivery of packages and letters for customers.
Summer 2003

YOUTH CONSERVATION CORPS, Reno, NV
Maintenance Worker
* Involved with upkeep and improvement of state park trails.
* Constructed fence to protect state park nature preserve.
Summer 2002

CHARLIE'S BAR AND GRILL, Reno, NV
Busboy
* Cleared tables.
* Replenished supplies as needed.
Summers 1999 through 2001

ACTIVITIES
* Member, American Society of Civil Engineers.
* Member, National Eagle Scout Association.

PERSONAL
* Proficient with CAD and other Computer-Assisted Design programs.
* Willing to relocate.

REFERENCES: Available upon request.

JOSEPHINE ELIZABETH CROCKER
P.O. Box 317A • Trenton, NJ 08625
(609) 555-4832 • josephinecrocker@xxx.com

OBJECTIVE
To gain an entry-level position in the environmental health field with a firm that offers advanced training.

EDUCATION AND TRAINING
B.S., Environmental Health Science, Trenton State College, Trenton, NJ.
2001–2005.
3.2 GPA in major.

Courses
Principles and Practices of Environmental Health
Accident and Disaster Control
Technical Seminar in Environmental Health
Public Health Administration
Microbiology
Epidemiology
Health Biostatistics
Public Health Education
Administrative Seminar
Practicum in Environmental Health
Organic Chemistry
Applied Microbiology

Internships
- Internship, Vilas County Health Department, Environmental Division.
  May–August 2004.
- Internship, Oneida County Health Department, Environmental Division.
  May–August 2003.

AWARDS AND HONORS
- Intersorority Council Outstanding Greek Woman, 2004.
- *Who's Who Among Students in American Universities and Colleges*, 2004.
- Order of Chi Omega Greek Honorary, 2003.
- Society of Distinguished Collegiate Americans, 2002.

ACTIVITIES
- Chi Omega, President.
- Intersorority Council, Chief Justice of Judicial Board.
- United Cerebral Palsy Telethon, Phone Bank Coordinator.

References will be provided on request.

Cindy Miller

6652 E. Laurel Rd.
Newark, OH 43055
(614) 555-4331
C.Miller@xxx.com

CAREER OBJECTIVE
To secure a position emphasizing engineering and managerial skills with a firm engaged in building construction operations.

EDUCATION
Rutgers - The State University of New Jersey
College of Engineering, New Brunswick, NJ
Bachelor of Science
May 2004
GPA: 3.5/4.0
Major: Construction Engineering and Management
Significant Courses:
- Construction Estimating
- Construction Scheduling
- Computer Programming (SQL, Perl, and Html)
- Construction Management
- Labor Relations
- Finance and Accounting
- Technical Graphics
- Surveying

Curriculum focused on group projects: Developed complete schematic design and preliminary construction plans for a real facility.

EMPLOYMENT EXPERIENCE
Granite Construction Company, Watsonville, CA
Field Engineer/Scheduler   Summer 2003   60 hours/week
Responsibilities:
- Project layout
- Project checkout
- Scheduling of job activities
- Organizational preparation

PAGE 1 OF 2

EMPLOYMENT EXPERIENCE (CONT'D)

Granite Construction Company, Birmingham, AL
Estimator   Summer 2002   48 hours/week
Responsibilities:
- Document distribution
- Quantity takeoffs from prints
- Data entry
- Conceptual takeoffs from sketches

Granite Construction Company, Fort Worth, TX
Field Engineer/Tracker   Summer 2001   40 hours/week
Responsibilities:
- Project layout
- Project checkout
- Tracking job progression
- Laborer

ACTIVITIES

- Associated Builders and Contractors: advertising committee
- Intramural team sports: volleyball and badminton

REFERENCES

Available upon request

SHARI T. LUISO   shari_luiso@xxx.net

Permanent Address	**Current Address**
256 Dove Lane	P.O. Box 1259
Tampa, FL 33614	Evanston, IL 60204
(813) 555-6901	(847) 555-3246

GOAL
To obtain an entry-level position working for the city of Chicago

EDUCATION
Northwestern University, Evanston, IL
Bachelor of Arts degree in Public Policy Studies, May 2004.
Course work: Macroeconomics, Microeconomics, Economic Analysis for Public Policy Making, Leadership and Policy Change, Policy Analysis for Public Policy Making, Managerial Effectiveness, Policy Choice and Value Conflict, Analytical Methods for Public Policy Making, Statistical Quantitative Political Analysis.

Université Paris Sorbonne, Paris, France, 2002–2003 academic year.
Course work: French language, art, and history.
Faculty Honors list, Spring 2003.

WORK EXPERIENCE
Council for Entrepreneurial Development, Chicago, IL, June 2003–present.
Management Intern. Oversee weekly "Entrepreneur's Page" in *Chicago Business Journal*: contact area business leaders to match article topics with knowledgeable authors, personally write additional pieces, edit and compile all contributions.

Chicago Business Journal, Chicago, IL, Summer 2001.
Advertising and Promotion Intern. Created advertisements, researched photographs for ads, sold advertising space, promoted the *Chicago Business Journal*, and prospected for new advertisers.

First National Bank, Evanston, IL, Summer 2000.
Cost-Cutting Analyst. Analyzed existing personal computer allocation and purchasing. Proposed, developed, and instituted cost-cutting measures for existing systems. Implemented technology purchasing procedures. Worked in Consumer Services Group, Country Corporate Office.

OUTSIDE INTERESTS
Northwestern Club Soccer, Treasurer, 2002.
Wayne Manor Selective House, Selection Committee and Social Chairman, 2002.
Intramural sports: soccer, basketball, flag football.

REFERENCES
Available upon request.

MARY WU

marywu@xxx.com • 4838 Mercy Street • Carmel, IN 46032 • (317) 555-2831

OBJECTIVE

To obtain employment as an accountant.

EDUCATION

Kalamazoo College, Kalamazoo, MI, 2004
B.A., Economics and Business Administration
GPA: 3.75/4.00

COURSE WORK

Economics, Managerial Accounting, Computer Science, Calculus, Linear Algebra, and Multivariable Calculus.

EXPERIENCE

6/04–present
Assistant to Public Relations Director. United States National Hard Courts, Indianapolis, IN. Type press releases, update draw sheets, file tournament and player data, and answer phones.

7/03–6/04
Tennis Instructor. Clay Junior High School, Carmel, IN. Evaluated players, developed lesson plans, and gave group instruction to children and adults.

5/02–8/02
Tennis Camp Instructor and Counselor. Kalamazoo College, Kalamazoo, MI. Instructed and supervised ranked junior players, organized personal help sessions, and evaluated students.

6/01–9/01
Medical Transcriber. Dr. Sam Perkins, Family Physician, Carmel, IN. Updated patients' files with information involving diagnosis and treatment, and answered phone calls.

ADDITIONAL INFORMATION

- Taking CPA Examination in Fall 2005.
- Junior member of the National Collegiate Athletic Association Division III runner-up varsity tennis team at Kalamazoo College.
- Member of Alpha Lambda Delta, a college freshman national honorary society.

REFERENCES

Will be provided upon request.

Sandra Singh

CURRENT ADDRESS
502 Sleigh Street
Stockton, CA 95211
(209) 555-2416
sandrasingh@xxx.com

PERMANENT ADDRESS
223 Lindsay Lane
Baltimore, MD 21217
(301) 555-2913

OBJECTIVE
To obtain a position as a financial analyst with an international bank

EDUCATION
University of the Pacific, Stockton, CA
B.A., Political Science, 2005
GPA: 3.3 on 4.0 scale; Dean's List, 2003–2004
Course work: Financial Accounting, Policy Analysis Methods, Statistical Analysis, Managerial Effectiveness, Economics, Calculus, Management, Labor Relations, and German

Spring 2004 in Berlin Program, University of the Pacific
Studied German Reformation, Art History

FINANCIAL EXPERIENCE
International Swap Dealers Association, New York, NY
Summer Associate, Summer 2004
Reported directly to executive director and senior staff at 200-member international trade association. Conducted extensive research on emerging markets and new derivative products. Planned and organized international swaps conference. Produced historical data trend analysis based on past interest rate and currency swap data.

University of the Pacific Auxiliary Finance Office, Stockton, CA
Senior Accounting Clerk, Summer 2003
Reconciled accounts receivable and payable. Collected past-due balances. Researched and responded to vendor inquiries via e-mail and telephone.

Prudential-Bache Securities, Boston, MA
Investment Broker Assistant, Summer 2002
Gained strong foundation in fundamental principles and practices of investment decision making. Helped broker analyze and interpret data relating to his clients' accounts.

OTHER EXPERIENCE

University of the Pacific Biology-Forestry Library, Stockton, CA
Library Assistant, Academic years 2002–2004
Responsible for operation of circulation desk and reserve collections as part of work-study program.

USA Today, **Arlington, VA**
Mail Clerk, Summer 2001
Sorted and delivered large volumes of incoming mail. Expedited the requests of top editors and management, including rush deliveries and special-handling packages.

INTERESTS

Camping, Fishing, Basketball, Coaching

SKILLS

Proficient in Microsoft Word, Access, Excel, PowerPoint, and website design. Fluent in German and French.

REFERENCES

Available upon request.

BRIAN KANEKO
briankaneko@xxx.com

PERMANENT ADDRESS
57 Rochester Way
Marietta, GA 30060
(404) 555-5445

PRESENT ADDRESS
P.O. Box 4855
Stanford, CA 94309
(650) 555-1007

OBJECTIVE

An entry-level position in construction management that will allow me to use my technical, organizational, and interpersonal skills to assist with project control tasks.

EDUCATION

Stanford University, Stanford, CA
Department of Civil Engineering
Master of Science Degree Candidate, May 2005
GPA: 3.2/4.0

Harvey Mudd College, Claremont, CA
School of Civil Environmental Engineering
Bachelor of Science Degree, May 2002
GPA: 3.9/4.0

COURSE WORK

Civil Engineering Materials, Construction Project Organization and Control, Risk Analysis and Management, Construction Management, Heavy Construction and Earthwork, Legal Aspects of the Construction Process, Decision Analysis in Construction

EXPERIENCE

Research Assistant, June 2003–Present
California Transportation Institution, Stockton, CA. Research several design- and construction-related areas of bituminous materials as part of the Strategic Highway Research Program, sponsored by the Federal Highway Administration.

EXPERIENCE (CONT'D)

Staff Engineer, Summers 2001–2002
Thompson Engineers, Marietta, GA. Assisted in the preparation of an operation and maintenance manual for a leachate treatment plant and provided support in the compilation and review of all operation- and maintenance-related submittals from the general contractor and all subcontractors.

ACHIEVEMENTS

- Engineer-in-Training (EIT) Certification
- Graduate Assistantship, Stanford University
- Dean's List, Department of Civil Engineering, Stanford University
- Dean's List, School of Civil Environmental Engineering, Harvey Mudd College

SKILLS

- Computer Languages: C/C++, Visual Basic, Perl, SQL
- Computer Applications: Lotus SmartSuite, Excel, SAS, AutoCAD, Adobe Photoshop
- Fluent in Japanese

REFERENCES

Available upon request

BEVERLY M. LEBLANC

P.O. Box 8175 • Creighton University • Omaha, NE 68178
(402) 555-3686 • beverly.leblanc@xxx.com

OBJECTIVE

Environmental engineer position that involves the design of wastewater/water treatment systems, groundwater quality, remediation, groundwater modeling, and hazardous wastes site investigation.

EDUCATION

Creighton University—Omaha, NE
Master of Science in Engineering—2005
Major: Environmental Engineering
Overall GPA: 3.64/4.00
Major GPA: 3.84/4.00

University of Minnesota—Minneapolis, MN
Bachelor of Science in Engineering—2003
Major: Mechanical Engineering

TECHNICAL SKILLS

- Major Advanced Courses: Water Quality Analysis, Water Treatment Plant Design, Land Treatment of Wastes, Wastewater Treatment Plant Design, Industrial Wastes Treatment, and Sanitary Engineering
- Computer Languages: Visual Basic, COBOL MVS, SQL, Perl, Html, XML
- Operating Systems: MS DOS/MVS; Windows 95, 98, and NT; OS/390
- Hardware: AS 400
- Software: Word, SAS, Oracle Database

EXPERIENCE

Fall 2003—present   Graduate Research Assistant
Environmental Engineering Department
Creighton University
Monitor the operating and treatment efficiency of rotating biological contractors.

Summer 2002   Programmer
Environmental Engineering Department
University of Minnesota
Assisted in development of water treatment system.

Summer 2001   Operator
Minneapolis–St. Paul Wastewater Treatment Plant
Minneapolis, MN
Monitored routine operation of facility.

EXPERIENCE (CONT'D)
Summer 2000   Laboratory Analyst
Science Department
University of Minnesota
Assisted technicians on both short- and long-term projects.

ACTIVITIES
Member of Civil Engineering Honor Society
Student member of the National Society of Professional Engineers
Student member of the American Society of Civil Engineers

REFERENCES
Will be provided on request.

KELLY JOHNSON

546 Balstrode Way
Des Moines, IA 50312
(515) 555-2376
KJohnson@xxx.com

OBJECTIVE
To obtain a part-time position working in either a restaurant or a retail store.

EDUCATION
St. John's High School, 2004
GPA 3.00/4.00
My future educational plans are to attend a four-year state college.

COURSE WORK
Calculus, Keyboarding, Introduction to Business, and Spanish.

AFFILIATIONS
Girls' High School Swim Team.
Interact -- A community service club.
- Area Representative -- Senior.
- Vice President -- Junior.
- Community Commissioner -- Sophomore.
- Secretary -- Freshman.

WORK EXPERIENCE
4/03 - present
Round Table Pizza, Cook and Server.
Assemble pizzas, serve customers and take their orders, answer phones, and clean the restaurant.

6/02 - 8/02
Prairie Landscapes, Receptionist.
Answered phones and typed memos.

Weekends
Babysitting.

OTHER EXPERIENCE
Studied Spanish for five years and can act as a translator.

OUTSIDE INTERESTS
Reading, playing the piano, and swimming.

REFERENCES
Available upon request.

HEATHER MORENO

48 Hickory Drive
Houston, TX 77002
(713) 555-4968
heathermoreno@xxx.net

OBJECTIVE:	To obtain a position in the secretarial field.
EDUCATION:	Victoria High School, 2005 GPA 3.80/4.00 ■ I plan to attend Texas Southern University and major in Business.
COURSE WORK:	■ Keyboarding ■ Accounting ■ Mathematics ■ Introduction to Personal Computers & Web Design ■ Psychology
ACTIVITIES:	■ Council Member of Victoria High School Student Government ■ Lead dancer of Flamenco Dance Group ■ Organizer of youth group meetings for Christian Fellowship
WORK EXPERIENCE:	6/04–12/04 Patterson Prizes, Inc., Receptionist ■ Job entailed answering the phone, entering names into a computer, cleaning, and lifting boxes.
INTERESTS:	■ Jogging ■ Dancing ■ Reading ■ Cooking
REFERENCES:	Available upon request.

ANTHONY J. RUELAS

364 Sidewinder Way
Lubbock, TX 79409
(806) 555-0923
anthony.ruelas@xxx.com

POSITION DESIRED

Political Aide

EDUCATION

Lubbock High School, 2004
GPA 3.70/4.00
I plan to attend a four-year university.

COURSE WORK

Political Science I, II
World History
Computer Science I, II
Advanced Speech

ACTIVITIES

Associated Student Body, president
Student Council, representative
Special Education Community Advisory Committee, member

WORK EXPERIENCE

OFFICE ASSISTANT, Summer 2004
Network Real Estate

PAGE, September 2003–February 2004
Texas House of Representatives

REFERENCES

Upon request

CRISTINA GONZALES

98 Freedom Blvd. • Seattle, WA 98122 • (206) 555-4691 • C.Gonzales@xxx.com

POSITION DESIRED
A salaried community service position enabling me to work with and help others.

EDUCATION
Seattle High School, 2004
GPA 3.50/4.00; four-year member of honor society

I plan to attend a four-year university to obtain a degree in Psychology.

SCHOOL ACTIVITIES
- Sophomore class president
- Student Organization member
- Commissioner of Hospitality
- Soccer team member
- Softball team member

OUTSIDE INTERESTS
- Writing/Weblogging (blogging)
- Soccer
- Softball
- Reading
- Swimming

SKILLS
- Speak fluent Spanish.
- Type 40 words per minute.

WORK EXPERIENCE
Wal-Mart, Seattle, WA
Merchandise cashier
5-02 to 9-04

REFERENCES
Available upon request.

NATHAN MOYA

562 York Avenue South • Beaverton, OR 97005
(503) 555-4159 • nathan.moya@xxx.com

GOAL

To display my diligent work ethic while gaining solid work experience.

EDUCATION

Beaverton High School, 2004
GPA 3.50/4.00
I plan to attend a four-year university and law school.

COURSE WORK

Leadership class--organization, leadership, responsibility
Geometry--abstract thinking
Spanish--fluency in another language

ACTIVITIES

Swim Team
Track-and-Field Team
Student Trustee to the School Board
Member--Associated Student Body
Boy Scouts Life Rank
Volunteer--AIDS Quilt, 2003
Volunteer--Food Bank, 2002

INTERESTS

Swimming
Backpacking
Running
Hiking
Cycling

SKILLS

Fluent in Spanish language
Computer literate--Mac OSX and Windows ME and XP

WORK EXPERIENCE

McDonald's, Summer 2004. Efficiently served customers with a positive attitude.
Ed's Upholstery, 2002 - 2003. Dependably picked up and delivered furniture, cleaned shop.

REFERENCES

Available on request

MARYBETH A. WHITTLE

5679 Opal Cliff   Edmonds, WA 98020   (206) 555-2177
marybeth_whittle@xxx.com

GOAL

To obtain a position in which I can demonstrate
my ability to handle challenging tasks.

EDUCATION

Edmonds High School, 2004
GPA 3.80/4.00
Next year I will be attending Georgetown University.
After completing my college education, I plan to enter law school.

SCHOOL ACTIVITIES

Cheerleading
Associated Student Body--Secretary
Site Council Member
Key Club--Community service club member

WORK EXPERIENCE

Jennifer's Bakery--cash register, cleaning
Summers 2002, 2003

INTERESTS

Running
Knitting
Maintaining my website

PERSONAL

I am a responsible individual who enjoys working with others.

REFERENCES

Available upon request

ELIZABETH M. LEIGH-WOOD
387 Sunny Hills Drive
Madison, WI 53711
(608) 555-1524
e.leigh-wood@xxx.net

OBJECTIVE
A position as a lifeguard.

EDUCATION
Madison High School, 2004
GPA 3.80/4.00
+ General education/Honors classes
+ Next fall I will be attending Cardinal Stritch University in Milwaukee, WI,
  on a track scholarship.

SCHOOL ACTIVITIES
+ Four-year member of Associated Student Body Council
+ Four-year member of Wisconsin Scholarship Federation
+ Four-year member of Varsity Track Team
+ Two-year member of Varsity Swim Team

SKILLS
+ Fully trained as lifeguard
+ Certified in Standard First Aid and CPR
+ Fluent in French
+ Hardworking and outgoing

WORK EXPERIENCE
+ Hospital volunteer, 2003–2004
+ American Cancer Society volunteer Christmas gift wrapper, 2002–2004
+ Whalers' Car Wash, 5/03–10/03
+ Lifeguard, Sunny Hills Neighborhood Club, 5/02–8/02
+ Babysitting, weekends

REFERENCES
Upon request

SERENA STRELITZ

645 Doris Avenue

Salt Lake City, UT 84112

(801) 555-0211

serena.strelitz@xxx.com

OBJECTIVE
I am seeking a job in clothing or food sales.

EDUCATION
Salt Lake City High School, 2004
GPA 3.25/4.00
General education/Honors and Advanced Placement classes
I will be attending Brigham Young University, Provo, UT, during the next academic year. I plan to obtain a Master's degree in Communication.

SKILLS
- Fluent in Spanish
- Hardworking
- Congenial worker

WORK EXPERIENCE
Farm Bakery—salesperson
November 2002 to present

Snack Shack at football games—salesperson, cashier, and cook
August to October, 2000 to 2004

SCHOOL ACTIVITIES
- Three-year member of Interact, a community service club
- Three-year member of Key Club, a community service club
- Four-year member of Utah Scholarship Federation, including one year as president
- Two-year member of Varsity Track Team

VOLUNTEER WORK
I spent one year as an assistant in a first-grade class, 2003.
I worked on a political campaign to elect a state representative in 2002.

REFERENCES
Available upon request

MATTHEW BERDAL
351 Huntington Drive
Jacksonville, FL 32211
(904) 555-5050
mberdal@xxx.net

GOAL
A position using my skills as a specialist in PC software training and network support.

QUALIFICATIONS
- Expert troubleshooter and problem solver.
- Proven ability to educate and motivate others.
- Proficient in PC software and hardware.

EDUCATION
Jacksonville University, Jacksonville, FL, 2004
Major—Computer Science, GPA 3.8/4.0

TRAINING
- Visual Basic
- Programming
- DEC—PCSA/VAX Based Server System Management
- DEC—Network Management I
- DEC—VAX/VMS System Management I
- SQL
- Oracle Database
- Html, XML, PHP, and other Web programming languages

EMPLOYMENT HISTORY
INFO TEC Video Systems, Jacksonville, FL
PC Specialist, 2002–present
Programmer, 2001

Bob's Family Market, Jacksonville, FL
Manager, 2000

PROFESSIONAL EXPERIENCE
- Act as administrator for ALL-IN-1 electronic mail on a VAX 4000, with the integration of PC word-processing documents and spreadsheets.

PROFESSIONAL EXPERIENCE (CONT'D.)

- Repair and upgrade all components of PC hardware: Compaq, AST, IBM, AT&T, HP, Epson, Dell, and Gateway.
- Provide technical consulting to managers demonstrating comprehensive awareness of staff needs.
- Train PC users nationwide via telephone.
- Instruct company personnel on an individual basis.
- Design and present training classes on PC software, DOS, and OC fundamentals.

REFERENCES

Available upon request.

MARVIN HOPKINS

marvinhopkins@xxx.com
341 Beach Pines Drive
Olympia, WA 98505
(206) 555-2397

OBJECTIVE

To work as a project engineer with a computer manufacturer and advance to a management position in research and development.

EDUCATION

Eastern Washington University, Cheney, WA
B.S., Computer and Information Sciences, 2005

TECHNICAL SUMMARY

Software:
> Lotus SmartSuite, WordPerfect, TCP/IP, Microsoft Office (Excel, PowerPoint, Word, Access), and Windows Explorer.

Hardware:
> Windows-compatible personal computers, Macintosh computers, laser/inkjet printers, modems, plotters, scanners, and AS/400.

Languages:
> Visual Basic, COBOL MVS, DB2, Oracle Databases, and SQL.

SUMMER WORK EXPERIENCE

2003, 2004

> **Microsoft, Redmond, WA**
> - Assistant Systems Manager—Member of four-person team that installed and implemented a 60-node 3Com 3Plus local area network, including 53 IBM-compatible personal computers and nine Macintosh computers. Provided support for WordPerfect, Lotus SmartSuite, and electronic mail.

2002

> **MCCAW Cellular Communications, Kirkland, WA**
> - Programmer and Educator—Provided support for all aspects of Windows-compatible personal computers, including software.

REFERENCES

Work and education references on request.

Willing to relocate.

S A R A H   L O U I S E   H I L L

865 Woodside Drive • Chattanooga, TN 37403
(615) 555-0469 • sarah.hill@xxx.com

P R O F E S S I O N A L   O B J E C T I V E
To gain a position as a marketing representative with possibility of advancement into management.

E D U C A T I O N
UNIVERSITY OF TENNESSEE
Chattanooga, TN
B.S., Business Administration, anticipated May 2005

E X P E R I E N C E
Summers 2003, 2004
UNION PLANTERS CORPORATION OF AMERICA
Nashville, TN
Sales Representative: Responsible for service and sales in the Nashville area. Increased sales by 5 percent each summer. Awarded the 2004 Murphy's Trophy for achieving sales expectancy in every product line.

Summer 2002
HEALTHTRUST
Nashville, TN
Sales Representative: Achieved 150 percent of expected quota for June to August, calling on business and industrial accounts in Tennessee. Ranked first out of 12 salespeople.

Summer 2001
A & P SUPERMARKET
Nashville, TN
Cashier.

C O M P U T E R   E X P E R I E N C E
Word, Access, Excel, PowerPoint.

H O B B I E S   A N D   I N T E R E S T S
Golf, softball, family activities, travel, volunteer work.

R E F E R E N C E S
References will be provided upon request.

Willing to relocate.

RACHEL DURAN
rachelduran@xxx.com

298 Cass Street
Salem, OR 97309
(503) 555-5329

P.O. Box 1048
Eugene, OR 97405
(503) 555-5917

OBJECTIVE

To serve as a receptionist in the executive suite of a large corporation.

EDUCATION

Lane Community College, Eugene, OR, 2004
Degree—Business and Office Technician

ACHIEVEMENTS

- Lane Community College Dean's List, December 2003
- Lane Community College "Student of the Month," October 2003
- Certificates of Achievement for Accounting, English, and Spelling
- Oregon Girls' State Representative, 2001
- Student Body Treasurer, Salem High School, 2001–2002
- Who's Who on the West Coast, 2001 edition

SKILLS

- Computer: MS Word, Access
- Machine transcription
- Typing: 85 wpm

EXPERIENCE

RECEPTIONIST—U.S. BankCorp, Portland, OR, Summers 2002, 2003.
Job included: typing, filing, and processing mail.

RECEPTIONIST—William H. Schmeida, M.D., Salem, OR, Summer 2001.
Job included: handling monthly reports, typing, processing mail, and filing general correspondence material.

REFERENCES

Available upon request

NOLAN T. YU
nolanyu@xxx.com

PRESENT ADDRESS
P.O. Box 61434
Cambridge, MA 02139
(617) 555-6087

PERMANENT ADDRESS
1534 Elm Street
Catonsville, MD 21228
(301) 555-6053

OBJECTIVE
To obtain a position in finance or consulting that requires technical expertise.

EDUCATION
MASSACHUSETTS INSTITUTE OF TECHNOLOGY, Cambridge, MA
B.S., Computer and Information Sciences
June 2004
GPA: 3.5/4.0

EXPERIENCE
MIT BOOKSTORE
Loss Prevention Agent, February–June 2004
Coordinated shrinkage control system, which included the compilation of monthly reports on loss prediction data and statistics. Division reduced inventory loss due to theft by 12 percent.

MIT DINING SOCIETY
Financial Manager, September 2002–June 2003
Coordinated a quarterly budget of $65,000. Investigated and analyzed budgetary problems. Revised financial accounting system and established mechanisms for the analysis of fiscal progress through implementation of a database management software system.

SKILLS
• PC and Macintosh—Windows ME & XP; Mac OSX; MS Office: Excel, Word, Access, Outlook Express
• Fluent in Chinese (Mandarin)

ADDITIONAL INFORMATION
• MIT Engineering Association
• MIT Prebusiness Society
• Varsity tennis team, 2001–2002

References available upon request

HANK MADRUGA

243 Shoreview Way
Minneapolis, MN 55454
(612) 555-7080
H.Madruga@xxx.com

OBJECTIVE

To become a salesclerk in a major department store.

WORK EXPERIENCE

December 2003 - present

Pete's Deli-Café
Minneapolis, MN
General helper: Responsible for operating cash register, taking food orders, doing dishes, catering, ordering and stocking supplies, dealing with the public, and preparing some food.

March 2002 - December 2003

Common Ground Books & Coffee
Minneapolis, MN
Barista & cashier: Prepared a wide variety of coffee drinks. Served customers with a pleasant attitude and knowledge of coffee drinks.

OTHER EXPERIENCE

- Member, Lakeside High School newspaper staff
- Member, Lakeside High School ski club
- Member, Lakeside High School baseball team
- Member, Lakeside High School swim team
- Member, Lakeside High School track-and-field team
- Member, Lakeside High School cross-country team

EDUCATION

Lakeside High School, Minneapolis, MN, 2004

REFERENCES

Will be made available upon your request.

Loretta M. Alston

305 Doris Avenue • Baldwin City, KS 66006 • (913) 555-0211
loretta_alston@xxx.com

◈ Objective

To obtain a position in which my secretarial skills, my organizational abilities, and my willingness to assume responsibility can be employed.

◈ Education

Baker University; Baldwin City, KS, 2004
Major: English Literature

◈ Experience

Summers 2002–2003
REINHARDT & ASSOCIATES LAW CORPORATION
Baldwin City, KS
Personal Secretary for Michael J. Green
* Composed and prepared correspondence
* Handled accounts receivable
* Performed receptionist and general secretarial duties

Summer 2001
SPEEDO INC.
Baldwin City, KS
Secretary
* Performed data entry on PC
* Maintained mailing list database
* Purchased office supplies

Summers 1999–2000
EXECUTIVE SUNN CENTERS
Baldwin City, KS
Receptionist
* Maintained company switchboard

◈ Additional Information

I am familiar with Microsoft Windows XP, Microsoft Office 2003, and WordPerfect. I can type 81 words per minute.

◈ References

Available upon request

CHARLES P. BHATIA

Campus Address
P.O. Box 7327
Henniker, NH 03242
(603) 555-7123

Permanent Address
234 Rose Street
Greenville, IL 62246
(618) 555-4335

OBJECTIVE

To obtain a part-time position in manufacturing, analysis, or project development.

EDUCATION

New England College, Henniker, NH
Pursuing B.S. in Industrial Engineering, expected 6/05.
GPA: 3.5/4.0.
Responsible for 20 percent of college expenses.

EXPERIENCE

6/04–9/04
Management Engineering Intern
Greenville Health Center, Greenville, IL
Analyzed work flow and made procedural recommendations to hospital administrator. Built computerized daily productivity report and employee database file converters. Led team in continuous process improvement project, which involved extensive interviewing.

1/02–6/03
Student Manager
Bon Appétit, Henniker, NH
Interviewed and trained new and current employees. Scheduled workers and reduced labor costs significantly. Planned strategies with director of retail. Changed and improved products. Inventoried and ordered food products weekly. Served and cashiered.

ACTIVITIES

8/04–5/05
Student Government Association Member
Henniker, NH
Coordinated survey of 2,000 undergraduate classes as assistant director of course evaluations. Debated proposed legislation as the representative for the undergraduate academic council. Oversaw student election process on the ethics committee.

9/03–6/05
Urban Community Vision Volunteer
Henniker, NH
Tutored underprivileged children weekly at their schools. Organized children's retreat.

COMPUTER SKILLS

Computer knowledge includes SAS, WordPerfect, Lotus 1-2-3, Excel, Access, programming in C++.

REFERENCES

Available upon request.

VICTORIA ALEXANDER FLYNN

ADDRESS
4678 Freedom Boulevard
Newark, DE 19716

TELEPHONE
(302) 555-4780

E-MAIL
victoria.flynn@xxx.com

CAREER OBJECTIVE
A growth-oriented position in Human Resources Management

EDUCATION
University of Delaware, Newark, DE
Master's in Business Administration, 2004

Goldey Beacom College, Wilmington, DE
B.S., Business and Management, 2002

SUMMER EXPERIENCE
2002 and 2003
KELSEY TECHNOLOGIES CORPORATION
Member of team whose responsibilities included
- Contingency plan development/implementation
- Administration of various salaried benefit programs
- Hourly and salaried technical training
- Salary planning

2000 and 2001
NEWARK PUBLIC SCHOOLS
Teacher's aide whose responsibilities included
- Instruction of Business Law, Business Management, and Accounting to high-school juniors and seniors
- Curriculum development

ADDITIONAL INFORMATION
- Excellent skills in MS Word and Access
- Four Varsity Letters in field hockey, Goldey Beacom College
- Three Varsity Letters in track and field, Goldey Beacom College
- Assistant coach, Wilmington High School field hockey team

REFERENCES
Available upon request

CRAIG L. HJORRING

31 Anderson Road • Fort Collins, CO 80523
(303) 555-0469 • craig.hjorring@xxx.com

OBJECTIVE

Management position with emphasis in Marketing and Sales.

EDUCATION

Colorado State University, Fort Collins, CO
B.S. in Business Administration and Management expected May 2005
GPA 3.49/4.00

MEMBERSHIPS

Society of Manufacturing Engineers
Fabricating Manufacturers Association

EXPERIENCE

Sutherland Sports Wear
Assistant Regional Sales Manager
Summers 2002–2004

ACHIEVEMENTS

• Orchestrated and created all sales literature and advertising, which decreased advertising costs from 8.5 percent to 2.4 percent of sales.

• Increased sales from June to August more than 20 percent each summer.

• Acquired industry contacts providing for joint ventures with suppliers and customers as member of sales team.

PERSONAL

I enjoy biking, swimming, and family activities.

REFERENCES

Available upon request.

PHILIP E. GADBAW
P.Gadbaw@xxx.com

1625 South Sylvester Street
Crestview Hills, KY 41017
(606) 555-2368

P.O. Box 9087
Bowling Green, KY 42101
(502) 555-9851

OBJECTIVE
A position in product/brand marketing that offers exposure to product planning and development, market research, and advertising.

EDUCATION
Master of Business Administration, May 2005
Western Kentucky University
GPA 4.00/4.00
> A broad graduate program in Marketing and Finance, supported by course work in Management, Business Planning, Operations, Economics, and Accounting.

Bachelor of Science degree in Industrial Engineering, May 2003
Glenville State College
> Extensive course work in Economics, Mathematics, Statistics, and Communication Arts.

EXPERIENCE
Liberty National Bancorp
Louisville, KY
Summers 2003, 2004
Industrial Engineer
> Designed, performed, and presented factory and office productivity studies with measured savings in excess of $200,000 per study. Accomplishments included the successful engineering, organizing, and presenting of projects and layouts involving expenditures up to $300,000.

Humana
Louisville, KY
Summer 2002
Packaging Engineer
> Initiated cost savings for June to August period.

Circuit City Stores
Glenville, WV
Summer 2001
Engineering Internship
   Responsibilities included routing, structuring of bill materials, and supervising hourly employees.

REFERENCES
Available upon request.

CHRISTOPHER J. HEALY

142 Peachtree Lane
Montgomery, AL 36193
(205) 555-9484
cjhealy@xxx.com

OBJECTIVE

To obtain a position within a marketing or general management firm.

EDUCATION

FAULKNER UNIVERSITY, Montgomery, AL, 2005
Associate's degree in Business Administration and Management
Bachelor's degree in Accounting
GPA 4.00/4.00

HONORS
• Beta Gamma Sigma
• Business/Management Honorary
• Accounting Honorary

PART-TIME WORK EXPERIENCE

Head Coach for Montgomery Summer Basketball League.
Organized and directed four winning teams, including Sectional and Cluster Champions.
June to August, 2003 and 2004

Assistant Coach for Montgomery Summer Basketball League.
June to August, 2002

Waiter at Max's Grill.
Primarily served food, occasionally helped to clean and clear tables.
June to August, 1999, 2000, and 2001

REFERENCES

Furnished upon request.

NICOLE ANNE CHANG

3089 McGlenn Drive • Jonesboro, AR 72402
(501) 555-9268 • nicole.chang@xxx.net

OBJECTIVE

Position as a veterinary hospital manager.

EDUCATION

Arkansas State University, Jonesboro, AR, 2004
B.S. in Biology
GPA 3.45/4.00

AWARDS

Member of Dean's List, 2004
All-Academic Soccer Team, 2003
High School All-American Soccer Player, 2000

EXPERIENCE

Veterinarian Assistant Volunteer, Michael Stein's Veterinary Hospital.
June to August, 2002 to 2003
Assisted with the administration of medicine and pacification of the animals.

Assistant Coach, Jonesboro Summer Soccer League.
June and July, 1996 to 1999

PERSONAL

I am a very patient and caring person.
I love working with animals.
I am willing to relocate.

References on request.

CHRISTOPHER M. ISENBRAND
2711 Mar Vista Drive
Farmington, CT 06032
(203) 555-8900
christopher_isenbrand@xxx.com

OBJECTIVE

A position as a technician or an assembler.

BACKGROUND SUMMARY

Have demonstrated analytical, technical, and managerial skills. Communicate effectively with corporate representatives and government inspectors. Able to think in an objective manner. Possess excellent problem-solving skills. Work habits are clean, efficient, and organized.

EDUCATION

U.S. Navy
Avionics Electronics classes (equivalent to A.A. degree)

Central Connecticut State University, New Britain, CT, 1995
B.S., Engineering Technology
Minor: Manufacturing Technology
GPA: 3.56/4.00

EXPERIENCE

U.S. Navy, Aviation Electrician, 1995–2004
Received an Honorable Discharge.

PERSONAL

I have lived in Hawaii and Japan and have acquired Japanese language skills.

REFERENCES

Available upon request.

MELISSA L. JUNG
1530 Hansen Lane
Dover, DE 19901
(302) 555-9401
melissa.jung@xxx.net

OBJECTIVE:

To secure employment as an elementary education teacher.

EDUCATION:

University of Delaware, Newark, DE, 1989
M.A., Education
GPA 3.50/4.00

Wesley College, Dover, DE, 1987
B.A., Elementary Education
GPA 3.90/4.00

VOLUNTEER EXPERIENCE:

- Assistant art teacher, Dover Elementary School.
- Five-year member, Dover Rotary Club.
- Head of fund-raiser that raised $54,000 to finance a new local elementary school.
- Volunteer at local soup kitchen once a week.
- Hostess for six exchange students from France, Germany, and Japan.

PERSONAL:

- I have been a homemaker since 1990.
- I am the mother of four children.
- I assist my husband in his business by delivering merchandise, purchasing supplies, and arranging financing.
- I enjoy swimming, biking, and traveling.

REFERENCES:

Available upon request.

LARRY LAWSON JONES
6542 Jackson Blvd.
La Mesa, CA 91941
(619) 555-3428
larry.jones@xxx.com

EMPLOYMENT OBJECTIVE
A career in aviation, beginning as pilot of a commercial single- or twin-engine plane.

SUMMARY
Graduate of the University of California, Irvine, with a Bachelor of Arts degree in Economics. Supplemented a challenging academic program with flying and sailing. Received a private pilot's license and competed in college sailing.

EDUCATION
Aeronautical
American Flyers, San Diego, CA, Instrument Rating, October 2004.
Sunrise Aviation, Orange County, CA, Private Pilot's License, December 2003.

General
University of California, Irvine.
B.A., Economics, June 2004.

HONORS
Nominee, Scholar-Athlete, University of California, Irvine, 2004.
Collegiate All-American Sailor, 2003, 2004.

EXPERIENCE
Aeronautical
Currently working toward commercial rating.
Logged 240 hours, much of it complex, including transcontinental flights.

General
Sailing coach, University High School, San Diego, CA, 2002–2004.
Yacht racing clinic instructor for San Diego Yacht Club, 2002–2003.
Represented the United States at Japan/U.S.A. Goodwill Regatta, Tokyo, Japan, 2002.

REFERENCES
Will be made available on request.

HOWARD LUM

125 Apple Lane • Daytona Beach, FL 32015
(904) 555-8875 • howardlum@xxx.com

OBJECTIVE

A position in residential or commercial construction

EDUCATION

Broward Community College, Fort Lauderdale, FL, 2005
Major--Landscape Architecture

Daytona Beach High School, Daytona Beach, FL, 2003
Business track

PART-TIME WORK EXPERIENCE

June to August, 2002 to 2004
Florida State Insulation Co.--Daytona Beach, FL
> Started as a laborer and worked up to the position of assistant
> foreman of a five-person crew. Responsible for previewing jobs,
> supplying material, and performing residential and commercial
> insulation applications.

June to September 2001
Simmons Roofing Company--Daytona Beach, FL
> Performed all phases of hot asphalt and shingle roofing on both
> commercial and residential properties.

PERSONAL

I am a very diligent and hardworking individual who has the ability to
give and receive directions effectively.

My hobbies include fishing and water skiing.

REFERENCES

Available upon request

MAXWELL Y. KITYAMA

4200 Birch Lane
Rome, GA 30163
(404) 555-5450
M.Kityama@xxx.com

OBJECTIVE

Full-time employment as a mechanic

EXPERIENCE

BUTLER MACHINERY, Rome, GA
Summers 2001 to 2004
Manufacturer of correct mechanical components for high technology

Set up the operation of machine tools, including lathes, milling machines, drill presses, and grinders. Experienced with precision measuring instruments; fabrication procedures including welding, sheet metal, and casting; and implementation of documentation conventions for dimensions, tolerance, and finishing.

PERSONAL

I am skilled in mechanics, carpentry, masonry, painting, and landscaping.
I enjoy playing golf and baseball.
I am a volunteer coach for the local high-school baseball summer league team.

EDUCATION

Floyd College, Rome, GA
A.S., Mechanical Engineering, 2004

Rome High School, Rome, GA
Specialty--Mechanics, 2002

REFERENCES

Full references will be furnished on request.

Roberto I. Martinez

1690 Sandy Lane
Marianna, FL 34619
(813) 555-7758
R.Martinez@xxx.com

Job Objective

• Technician/Assistant Engineer
• Industrial/Production Electronics

A position offering upward mobility in a quiet, professional environment. I am confident I can adapt successfully to the industrial/production environment. As a self-starter, I will learn whatever additional skills the position requires.

Part-Time Work Experience

Summer occupation 2001 to 2003, Marianna Radio/TV, Marianna, FL
TV, VCR, and Stereo Technician.

Summer occupation 2000, Allen TV Service, Marianna, FL
TV/Stereo Technician.

Summer occupation 1999, McDonald's restaurant, Marianna, FL
Food Server and Maintenance Worker.

Personal Evaluation

I am an electronics technician with a strong background in repairing consumer electronic products. I have designed and breadboarded many electronic devices, such as TTL circuits up to 14 ICs, audio special-effects projects, laser and power supply projects, security systems, infrared and ultrasonic measuring tools, and surface mount technology projects.

Education

Chipola Junior College, Marianna, FL, 2004
A.A. Equivalence Certificates in Electronics, AC/DC, Semiconductors, Circuits, Digital Electronics, and Microprocessors.

Marianna High School, Marianna, FL, 2002
General education.

REFERENCES ON REQUEST

EMILIA E. ALDRICH

1609 Poppy Way
Franklin Springs, GA 30639
(404) 555-0155
Cell: (404) 555-9987
emiliaaldrich@xxx.com

OBJECTIVE

A position in sales with the opportunity to reach the managerial level.

PERSONAL

- I always make an effort to complete scheduled projects successfully and on time.
- I am eager to learn and attentive to quality.
- I enjoy mountain biking, cooking, and fishing.

EXPERIENCE

City Market, Franklin Springs, GA. Checker/Stock Clerk. Duties included ordering of groceries and supplies, stocking shelves, cashiering, making weekly deposits to checking account, recording and submitting welfare vouchers, and taking inventory. Summers 2001, 2002, and 2003.

EDUCATION

Emmanuel College, Franklin Springs, GA, 2004
GPA 3.23/4.00
Major: Business and Office Studies.

Franklin Springs High School, Franklin Springs, GA, 2002
Educational focus on business courses.

REFERENCES

Available.

ROSAMARIA C. ALVAREZ

255 Outlook Drive ❖ Twin Falls, ID 83303
(208) 555-3242 ❖ Rosamaria.Alvarez@xxx.com

OBJECTIVE

A position as a senior or supervising receptionist providing efficient, high-quality typing, clerical, and word-processing services to a business firm.

EDUCATION

College of Southern Idaho, 2003
Certificate in Business Practices
Typing: 80 wpm
Office practice
Business machines

EXPERIENCE

Manpower Temporary Services, Twin Falls, ID
June to August 2000, 2001, and 2002
General office worker
- ❖ Filed applications, greeted applicants, and answered phones.
- ❖ Assisted with administration and grading of applicants' tests and completed all test paperwork.
- ❖ Gained experience in light invoicing, setting up files, typing, and data entry.

Idaho State Automobile Association, Twin Falls, ID
June to August 1999
Assistant cashier, relief PBX, and relief DMV
- ❖ Assisted customers with paperwork.
- ❖ Entered data in computer system.

COMPUTER EXPERIENCE

- ❖ Windows XP
- ❖ Microsoft Office 2003
- ❖ WordPerfect
- ❖ NEC PowerMate 8100 Series
- ❖ Microsoft Excel
- ❖ Microsoft PowerPoint

REFERENCES

Available upon request

Carrie King

704 Timberlake Court • Clinton, IA 52732 • (319) 555-1466
carrie.king@xxx.com

Objective
A full-time position as clerical assistant with the possibility of
advancement.

Education
Clinton Community College, Clinton, IA
Associate's degree, 2004

Course Work
* Microsoft Word 2003
* Microsoft Publishing
* Drafting
* Real Estate
* "Filing Efficiently" seminar
* "Take Charge Secretary" seminar

Experience
AEC Communications, Clinton, IA
Part-time Receptionist. 2002 - present
* Greet people and answer multilined telephone.
* Support office staff.

The Midwest Consumer, Clinton, IA
Personal Assistant. Summer 2001
* Assisted applicants and new employees with paperwork.
* Handled general office duties including filing.
* Assisted payroll occasionally.
* Kept notes of committee meetings.
* Assisted personnel manager with tasks including screening
  applicants and interviewing.

References will be provided upon request.

KEVIN R. LEE

46 La Mesa Drive   Coffeyville, KS 67337
(316) 555-1058   kevinlee@xxx.com

Summary

Technician experienced in assembly of electromechanical devices pertinent to cathode ray tubes. Experienced with soldering, welding, cleaning, and leak detection equipment. Familiar with most laboratory operations and tools, including conformance to process specifications and collecting/organizing data. Seeking a position that will allow me to utilize my skills.

Education

November 2002–November 2003
Coffeyville Control Data Institute, Coffeyville, KS
Completed 853-hour course in computer technology. Studies included basic and advanced electronics; digital logic and circuit analysis; Boolean algebra; CDC-Cyber 18-20 central processor; the 8080 microprocessor; hardware and software; peripheral equipment including card equipment, line printer, magnetic tape transport, and magnetic disc drive. Twenty percent hands-on time. Course also included extensive use of dual-trace oscilloscope multimeter logic trainers and visual display devices.

Experience

April 2001–October 2002
Mendelson Corporation, Coffeyville, KS
Test Technician
Tested and troubleshot a model 340 and a model 390 spectrophotometer. Performed tests on printed circuit boards and subassemblies.

Summers 1999, 2000
Your Market, Coffeyville, KS
Checker/Stock Clerk
Ordered groceries and supplies, took inventory, stocked shelves, cashiered, and recorded and submitted food stamp vouchers.

References
Available upon your request.

Sophia L. Krook

Address

746 Pineview Drive
Frederick, MD 21701
(301) 555-3121
sophia.krook@xxx.com

Objective

To use my education and experience in a challenging position in computer-based technical or customer support, with the potential for advancement.

Education

George Washington University, Washington, D.C.
B.A., Anthropology, 2004, with emphasis in Advertising
GPA 4.00/4.00

Awards

George Washington University Honors, 2004
Outstanding Academic Achievement, 2004
2003 Matt Arnerich Community Service Award

Areas of Expertise

I have the ability to combine a high level of customer relations and organizational skills with a sound analytical knowledge of technical line production and troubleshooting. I am computer literate in production and diagnostic testing using Hewlett Packard computers, frequency counters, spectrum analyzers, network analyzers, and power meters, among others.

Skills

I have self-taught PC familiarity and am well versed in Windows. I am skilled in Visual Basic, Oracle Database, and TCP/IP. Also, I am active on many bulletin boards and familiar with shareware and freeware in many categories.

References Available upon Request

Sabrina K. Lara

40065 Early Way • Boise, ID 83725 • (208) 555-9203 • sabrinalara@xxx.com

Objective	A position as a personal assistant.
Education	Boise State University, 1999–2000 Nine units toward Management Certificate Personnel Management Basic Supervision Computers in Management Professional office training (14 units) Business English, Math, and Machines Office Procedures Refresher Typing and Shorthand
Seminars	Accounting Principles (six units) Wage and Salary Administration Hiring and Firing EEOC Compliance
Skills	Work well with people. Excellent writing and organizational skills. Flexible and patient. Enjoy challenging and creative projects.
Interests	Reading, music (play flute and piano) Traveling and learning about other cultures
Experience	Self-Employed Assist in the publication of a monthly newsletter, "The Quaker Trails," and a quarterly one, "Let's Talk About Real Estate." Developed marketing materials for a realtor, including a "Career Portfolio" and a "Marketing Booklet" used to market individual listings. References will be provided upon request.

SIWA MSANGI

2590 Atlas Drive

Cedar Rapids, IA 52402

(319) 555-5850

siwa.msangi@xxx.net

OBJECTIVE
Full-time executive secretary appointment with the potential for advancement to personal assistant.

EDUCATION
Coe College, Cedar Rapids, IA
Bachelor of Arts, 2004
Major—Music
Minor—Art History and Appreciation
GPA 3.5/4.0

Cedar Rapids High School, 2000
Educational emphasis in Theater and Music

VOLUNTEER HISTORY
1999–2004
Des Moines Symphony Orchestra
Executive Secretary to President and Music Director
Provided administrative assistance. Prepared agendas and minutes of Board and Executive Committee meetings and scheduled meetings for fiscal year. Attended meetings for President. Maintained business and social calendars. Composed and transcribed correspondence. Supervised volunteers for special projects.

REFERENCES
Will be furnished upon request.

PENNIE L. PORTER
1730 Cowper Street
Parsons, KS 67357
(913) 555-9430
P.Porter@xxx.com

Objective
A position that will provide me with opportunities to learn and advance professionally in the IT field.

Education
Labette Community College, Parsons, KS
Associate's degree in Computer and Information Sciences, 2004

Parsons High School, 2002

Skills and Experience
Low Land Computer
2001 - 2004
As a volunteer in the family company, I have become experienced in all aspects of the processing of domestic shipments.
- Used UPS, Federal Express, and Airborne Express meter machines and Pitney Bowes U.S. Mail meter to dispatch and expedite truck shipments.
- Processed international shipments.
- Recorded and controlled all incoming and outgoing parts of the finished goods inventory.
- Performed data entry.
- Recorded supplies used in the traffic department and created purchase orders.

McDonald's
Summers 2000 - 2001
As opening cook, I became familiar with the process of making fast food.
- Prepared food to order.
- Restocked supplies to be used for the day.

References will be provided upon request.

LAURA KIRSTEN HUMMEL

529 Paul Revere Drive
Longmeadow, MA 01160
(413) 555-3093
laura.hummel@xxx.com

OBJECTIVE

A part-time job that will allow me to support myself while attending culinary school.

EDUCATION

Longmeadow High School, 2005
My scholastic GPA was 3.1/4.0.

FUTURE PLANS

I will attend Bay Path College and study food preparation and other culinary skills. I then plan to attend a university and major in Restaurant Management.

EXPERIENCE

The past three summers I have worked at Charlie's Deli Café in Longmeadow, MA. My duties included taking food orders, checking stock, preparing food, and operating the cash register.

PERSONAL

I was a two-year member of Longmeadow High's German Club.
I was a cheerleader at Longmeadow High for four years.
I am hardworking and dedicated.

TRANSPORTATION

I own a truck that can be used for transportation and work if necessary.

REFERENCES

Jay Johnson, Teacher, Longmeadow High School, (413) 555-0711, jayjohnson@xxx.com

Mary Hicks, Coach, Longmeadow High School, (413) 555-0711, maryhicks@xxx.com

FRANCINE P. SMITH

786 Quartz Street • Bangor, ME 04401 • (207) 555-8692
francine.smith@xxx.com

OCCUPATIONAL GOAL

I would like to become a dietician. Presently, I am seeking a part-time job that will allow me to attend school in order to prepare for my chosen field.

EDUCATION

High School: Bangor High School, Bangor, ME
Degree: High-school diploma, 2004
Grade point average: A-/B+

SPECIAL SKILLS

* I learn rapidly and work well with other people.
* I am skilled in word processing and using the Internet.

HOBBIES

* Exercising
* Skiing
* Playing the guitar

ACTIVITIES

* Member of the Bangor High School Key Club and American Field Service during my junior year.
* Member of the Bangor High School Concert and Marching Band during my freshman and sophomore years.

WORK EXPERIENCE

6/04–9/04
Child-care provider for 15 hours a week.

9/03–5/04
Housecleaner for three to four hours per week.

6/02–8/03
Babysitter for four to five hours a week.

REFERENCES

Available upon request.

Mitch L. DeLorenzo

29 Alta Dr.
Fulton, MS 38843
(601) 555-0331
mitch.delorenzo@xxx.com

Objective

I am very interested in obtaining employment that allows me to continually progress toward higher levels of performance. I am easily trained, a responsible employee, and a pleasant person to work with.

Education

I graduated from Fulton High School in 2005. My studies were concentrated in Economics and Business.

I have always been very active in sports. While at Fulton High School, I participated on the following athletic teams:
* Soccer team (four years; two years varsity).
* Track and cross-country team (three years).
* Swim team (one year).

During my senior year I was the financial manager of the varsity soccer team. This position taught me how to combine work and play.

I plan to attend Itawamba Community College for the next two years, where my studies will focus on Business Economics.

Experience

Joseph's Motor Home Service and Repair, Fulton, MS
June 1, 2003, to September 1, 2003

I was responsible for washing and repairing recreational vehicles. My job also included installing new accessories and appliances in motor homes.

References

Joseph Goode
Joseph's Motor Home Service and Repair
(601) 555-8965
joseph.goode@xxx.com

WILLIAM R. TANIMOTO

780 Weston Road
Mathiston, MS 39752
(601) 555-4194
Cell: (601) 555-7756
wrtanimoto@xxx.net

OBJECTIVE

A position as a part-time chef for the next two years with the potential
for a full-time position after graduation from college.

EDUCATION

Graduate of Mathiston High School, 2005
I plan to attend Wood Junior College in Mathiston, MS, starting fall 2005.

PERSONAL

Four-year member of the Mathiston High School baseball team.

Two-year member of the Adopt-a-Grandparent program
at the Convalescent Hospital in Mathiston.

Reliable and ready to work.

EXPERIENCE

Summers 2000–2004
JACOB'S RIB COMPANY, Mathiston, MS
- Preparing Food
- Cooking
- Operating cash register
- Preparing food backups
- Bussing tables
- Counting each day's receipts

REFERENCES

Will be made available upon request.

REBECCA C. PALMER

ADDRESS   345 Kingsbury Dr.
                      Hillsboro, MO 63050

TELEPHONE   (314) 555-8832

PROFESSIONAL   A permanent position as a receptionist or
OBJECTIVE   secretary in a well-established company
                      with good benefits and opportunities for
                      advancement

EDUCATION   Hillsboro High School, 2004

COURSE WORK   Shorthand   two semesters
                      Keyboarding   two semesters
                      Record Keeping one semester
                      Business Math   one semester

EXPERIENCE   Wendy's, Summer 2003
                      Crew Person:
                        Took customer orders
                        Cooked
                        Helped close the restaurant

REFERENCES   Available upon request

ANTHONY C. RUSSELL
----
762 E. 73rd St., Apt. 10C
New York, NY 10021
(212) 555-7310
anthony.russell@xxx.com

OBJECTIVE
Permanent employment in a kennel leading to a managerial position

----
EDUCATION
American Boarding Kennels Association: Completion of Stage One of the Home-Study Program, 2004

Park East High School, New York, NY, 2004

WORK EXPERIENCE
New York City Animal Shelter, 6/03 to present
- Assist in obedience training
- Provide basic animal health care
- Bathe and groom animals
- Answer telephone inquiries

Petco, 6/02 to 9/02
- Sold pet supplies
- Cleaned cages
- Fed and watered animals

Dog Walking, 4/00 to 5/02
- Walked six animals twice a day, Monday through Friday

PERSONAL
Own and show Mitzi, a four-year-old golden retriever

REFERENCES
Available upon request

PAULA MURRAY

308 Meredith Avenue
Missoula, MT 59812
(406) 555-3328
paula.murray@xxx.com

PROFESSIONAL OBJECTIVE

Employment as an aerobics instructor.

EDUCATIONAL BACKGROUND

2004 graduate of Missoula High School.

RELEVANT COURSE WORK

Physical Education	eight semesters
Human Relations	one semester
Psychology	one semester
Physiology	one semester

ACTIVITIES

Soccer	eight years
Swimming	four years
Basketball	two years
Softball	two years
Soccer Team Manager	two years

SUMMER EMPLOYMENT

1999–2004
YWCA Sports Camp, Missoula, MT
Head Counselor (2002–2004)   Assistant Counselor (1999–2001)
Responsible for children aged 6–12.
Directed aerobics program.

REFERENCES

Available upon request.

JOHN NOWARK

john.nowark@xxx.com
217 Arthur Avenue
Omaha, NE 68103
(402) 555-5003

Career Goal:	To secure a position as an assistant greenkeeper.
Education:	Dundee High School Graduate, 2005 General Education GPA 3.00/4.00 overall, 3.50/4.00 science

Science Classes:	Horticulture	two semesters
	Biology	two semesters

Art Courses:	Ceramics	one semester
	Basic Art, Drawing	one semester
	Digital Photography	one semester

Mathematics:	Algebra	two semesters
	Geometry	two semesters

Experience:	Summers 2003 to present Sugar Hill Nursery 453 Eureka Lane, Omaha, NE 69337 Nursery Assistant—Prepared nursery beds for planting. Watered, weeded, and sprayed trees, shrubs, and plants. Filled orders. Summers 1999 to 2002 4-H Camp 1500 Eureka Lane, Omaha, NE 69337 Counselor—Responsible for 20 children each year for one week in the month of July.
References:	Available upon request.

CAROL M. LEE
1389 Stevenson Road • Denver, CO 80221 • (303) 555-1275 • carollee@xxx.net

PROFESSIONAL OBJECTIVE
A position as a journalist in a firm that offers opportunities to use my writing skills.

EDUCATION
Graduate of Denver City High School, 2004
Major: English
GPA: 4.00 / 4.00
English Courses:
  American Literature
  Composition 1 and 2
  Dreams and Myths
  Short Story
  College English
  Shakespeare

EXPERIENCE
Golden Bear (school newspaper), Denver, CO
        Editor (2004)
        Reporter (2003)

The Coffee Pot, Denver, CO
        Administrative Assistant (March 2003 to present)
        Handle accounts receivable and computer input, file, and type.

Maude's Pantry, Denver, CO
        Cashier (August 2002 to February 2003)
        Waited on customers, answered the phone, restocked shelves, and priced merchandise.

PERSONAL
Currently writing and self-publishing a collection of short stories about my family's heritage as pioneers.

REFERENCES
Furnished upon request.

Matt J. Pointer
254 Vista Oaks
Glendive, MT 59330
(406) 555-8427

OBJECTIVE   A full-time position as an alarm technician in a firm with
                   opportunities for advancement.

EXPERIENCE   Assistant Alarm Technician
                   Primary Alarm
                   Part-time, 2001–2004
                   Assisted in the installation of various alarm systems for
                   large companies and private residences.

EDUCATION   Vista Oaks High School, graduated 2004
                   Relevant Course Work:
                   Keyboarding   two semesters
                   Business   two semesters
                   Office Skills   two semesters
                   Accounting   one semester
                   Communications   three semesters
                   Auto Shop   two semesters

REFERENCES   Jack Siri
                   P.O. Box 578
                   Glendive, MT 59330
                   (406) 555-4308
                   jacksiri@xxx.com

                   Anne Osorio
                   687 Creek Drive
                   Lame Deer, MT 59101
                   (406) 555-3105
                   anneosorio@xxx.com

ANGELA T. SANCHEZ

301 Coates Way
Alpena, MI 49707
(517) 555-8104
asanchez3@xxx.com

OBJECTIVE
Part-time position in communications that would use my past experiences while enabling me to continue my studies at Andrews University in Berrien Springs, MI. Position should include promotional possibilities.

EDUCATION
Alpena High School, 2003
I will attend Andrews University beginning in the fall of 2005. I plan to receive my Bachelor's degree in Communications in 2009.

WORK EXPERIENCE
June 2003 to Present
Customer Relations/Secretary
Jim's Audio Video Service Co.
Responsibilities: helping customers, filing, answering phones, ordering parts, and recording accounts payable and accounts receivable.

August 2002
Researcher
County Supervisors' Campaign Committee
Responsibilities: performing microfilm research.

June 2001 to August 2001
Office Assistant
Alpena Board of Realtors
Responsibilities: putting together and mailing newsletters, filing, and typing.

OTHER EXPERIENCE
- Member of varsity tennis and softball teams, 2002-2003.
- Member of yearbook staff--reporter and layout designer, 2002-2003.
- Member of Michigan Scholarship Association, 2001-2002.
- Proficient in Spanish.

REFERENCES
Available upon request.

GEORGIA R. HOLIDAY

576 Mesquite Drive
Waterville, ME 04901
(207) 555-8458
Mobile: (207) 555-7344
georgia.holiday@xxx.com

OBJECTIVE

To find a job that calls for learning and creativity and offers advancement in a friendly, people-oriented atmosphere.

EDUCATION

Waterville High School in Waterville, ME, graduated 2005
Grade Point Average 3.6/4.0

Areas of Concentration:
- English, four years
- Mathematics, four years
- Business Education, two years

WORK EXPERIENCE

The King's Service
Cleaning Service
2002 to 2005
Clerical Worker: Typed up work orders, filed, and answered business telephone.

The Perfect Place
Clothing Store
Summer 2002
Salesclerk: Sold clothing during sidewalk sales.

Floral Furnishings
Wholesale Florist Supply
Summer 2001
Clerical Worker: Wrote orders, did stock control, filed business papers, and answered business telephone.

REFERENCES AVAILABLE UPON REQUEST.

AARON C. KASAPI

aaron.kasapi@xxx.com • 276 Brooktree Ranch Rd.
Trinidad, CO 81082 • (719) 555-9335

Professional Objective
A position in architectural drafting with a construction company.

Education
Trinidad Public High School, 2003-2004
Graduated 2004

Stevenson High School, 2000-2003

Relevant Course Work
Woodshop	three years
Mechanical Drafting	one year
Math	three years
Architectural Drafting	two years
CAD (Computer-Assisted Design)	one year

School Sports
Wrestling	four years
Soccer	two years
Football	one year

Special Skills
• Creating computer graphics using Adobe Photoshop, Fireworks, and
  other digital design tools.
• Familiarity with layout programs, including Quark and PageMaker.
• Working knowledge of PowerPoint.
• Advanced word-processing applications.

Affiliations
"Out to Lunch Gang"--a band that played music during lunchtime at
high school.

Work Experience

6/04-8/04
Mountain Adventures, Boulder, CO
Assistant Guide
Helped tourists manage horses, raised tents, and assisted in meal preparation.

6/03-8/03
Taco Bell, Trinidad, CO
Crew Member
Prepared food and cleaned restaurant.

References

Will be made available upon request.

RITA J. FANG

304 Sierra Dr. • Los Angeles, CA 90069
(310) 555-0304 • ritafang@xxx.com

POSITION DESIRED
Restaurant cashier or hostess

EDUCATION
Galileo High School graduate, 2004
GPA 3.24/4.00

WORK EXPERIENCE
Bayview Restaurant, Los Angeles, CA
Title: Salad maker
Duties: Prepared salads and appetizers
Supervisor: Randy O'Neill
Dates: July to September 2003

Straw Hat Pizza, Los Angeles, CA
Title: Hostess, Cashier, Waitress, Busperson
Duties: Greeted customers, managed customer seating, answered the phone and took
        "to go" orders, operated a cash register and handled customers' money, served
        food, cleared tables, prepared salad bar, assisted in cooking of pizzas, and per-
        formed minimal maintenance chores
Supervisor: Marc Richards
Dates: August 2002 to May 2003

ACTIVITIES
* President, Galileo High School Scholarship Federation
* Member, Block A Club
* Member, Ski Gulls Club
* Member, volleyball and basketball teams

VOLUNTEER WORK
Los Angeles County Community Blood Bank
Title: Assistant
Duties: Comforted blood donors, served refreshments, and typed required donor forms

INTERESTS
Working with people in a social atmosphere
Personal physical development program

REFERENCES
Available upon request

JANICE E. KAHN

1005 Margaret St.   Willimantic, CT 06226
(203) 555-9203   janice_kahn@xxx.com

Objective

Part-time position as a gardener while I attend Eastern Connecticut State University.

School Attended

2005 Graduate of Willimantic High School
GPA 3.50/4.00

Academic Plans

To attend Eastern Connecticut State University in the fall of 2005 and major in Botany.

Specialty Classes

Regional Occupational Program course in Horticulture

Human Relations	one semester
Spanish	two years
Biology	two years
Keyboarding	one semester

Community Activities

Volunteer at the Mid-County Children's Center.

Hobbies and Interests

Playing the piano, gardening, crossbreeding flowers, running, and bicycling.

Work Experience

Magic Farms Nursery
June to August, 2002-2004
354 Floral Lane, Willimantic, CT 06226
Laborer--Packed and planted sprouts, changed and lifted racks, and filled and emptied sprout bins.

Part-time housecleaning
1999-2001

References

Will be made available upon request.

Douglas P. Shaw

191 Cuesta Way
Boise, ID 83706
(208) 555-8599
DPShaw@xxx.com

Objective
A position in the field of graphic arts or as a photographer

Education
Capitol High School, Boise, ID
Expected graduation date: 2005

Work Experience
Precious Moments Photography, Boise, ID
Photographic Assistant
Weekends 2000 to 2004
❯ Set up the lights and cameras
❯ Mixed chemicals
❯ Developed film and printed photographs

Jake's Chevron Station, Boise, ID
Daytime Laborer
Summers 2002 and 2003
❯ Handled two cash drawers, pumped gas, and made minor repairs
❯ Responsible for all bookkeeping on my shifts
❯ Kept garage area clean

Activities
Yearbook photography editor, 2004
Yearbook head photographer, 2003
Member, varsity soccer team, 2003
Member, junior varsity soccer team, 2002

Special Skills
Photography
Web page design
Dependability
Punctuality
Making clients feel comfortable

References will be made available upon your request

JARRON G. ADAMS
95 East 35th Street
Sioux City, IA 51103
(712) 555-9025
jarron.adams@xxx.net

GOAL
To work as an assistant manager in a pizza restaurant.

EDUCATION
Sioux City Central High School
Expected graduation date: 2005

EXPERIENCE
MAMA'S PIZZA—Sioux City, IA
Summer afternoons
Part-time during the school year

Food Preparation, 2004 to present
Wash dishes, bus tables, operate cash register, and make sandwiches.

Crew, 2002 and 2003
Made pizzas, bussed tables, washed dishes, operated cash register, and served customers.

ACTIVITIES
RED CROSS—Sioux City, IA
Volunteer Worker, 2004

INTERESTS
Skiing
Waterskiing
Camping
Reading
Hiking

REFERENCES
Furnished upon request.

Jeffrey R. Chuang

jeffreychuang@xxx.com
331 Hames Road
Belleville, IL 62221
(618) 555-5293

Objective
To become an automotive mechanic.

Education
Belleville High School--2004

Relevant Course Work
Mechanics 1 and 2
Auto Shop, two semesters
Accounting, two semesters

Experience
Summer 2003
Belleville Auto Body
Apprentice Bodyman
Prepared cars for painting, fixed dents, dismantled and reassembled various parts of vehicles, and washed cars.

Summers 2000-2002
Texaco
Station Attendant
Responsible for checking engine fluids, balancing tires, pumping gas, and related work.

Interests
Bike riding
Skiing
Music

Activities
Drummer for "The Fighting Fleas"
Amateur drag racing

References
Available upon request.

LISA P. CHINCHIOLO

7237 Hamman Drive • Chicago, IL 60606 • (312) 555-3368
lisa.chinchiolo@xxx.com

OBJECTIVE
A part-time position in a florist shop.

EXPERIENCE
2003–2004
Valley Ranch Homes
Maintained plants for model homes.

2001–2002
House and Lawn Care
• Did odd jobs for area houses.
• Mowed and watered lawns.
• Watched houses and pets.
• Did some landscaping and painting.

EDUCATION
Hamman High School, Chicago, IL
Expected graduation date: 2005
GPA 4.00/4.00
Plan to attend Loyola University, Chicago, IL.

SCHOOL ACTIVITIES
• Member of the Chicago Scholarship Federation. Attended all meet-
  ings and participated in activities.
• Four-year member of the Horticulture Club. Final year as President.

ADDITIONAL INFORMATION
I will graduate from Hamman High School as valedictorian with honors in science and have been named a National Merit Scholar.

REFERENCES WILL BE MADE AVAILABLE UPON YOUR REQUEST.

JOSEPH M. O'CONNELL

324 Encinal Avenue

Huntington, IN 46750

(219) 555-7419

joconnell@xxx.com

PROFESSIONAL OBJECTIVE
A position as a cashier/bagger with a company providing opportunities for advancement

EXPERIENCE
6/03 to present
ALBERTSON'S
145 Playa Boulevard
Huntington, IN 46750
My primary job was bagging; however, I also did some janitorial work.

6/02 to 9/02
PLAZA SHELL SERVICE
1872 41st Avenue
Huntington, IN 46750
My primary job was working as a cashier and completing the janitorial work.

EDUCATION
HUNTINGTON HIGH SCHOOL
Diploma, 2005

RELEVANT COURSE WORK
Mathematics	six semesters
Keyboarding	one semester
Computer Programming	one semester
Introduction to Business	one semester
English	six semesters

SCHOOL ACTIVITIES
Two-year member of the soccer team
Two-year member of the basketball team
Three-year member of the weight-lifting club

REFERENCES
Available on request

ELLY G. MINCH

245 Chaparral Drive
Chester, NH 03036
(603) 555-1364
EMinch@xxx.com

OBJECTIVE

To secure a part-time job as a cashier that will enable me to attend classes
and earn money to pay for my college education.

EDUCATION

Chester High School, 2005
764 Chaparral Drive
Chester, NH 03036
GPA 3.5/4.0

I will be attending Notre Dame College, Manchester, NH, in the fall of
2005. I plan to major in Psychology.

School Activities and Course Work:
• Business Education—two semesters.
• Keyboarding and Word Processing—two years.
• Varsity swim team member for three years—school's top swimmer.

WORK EXPERIENCE

May to July 2005
Cashier (part-time)
Baskin Robbins—ice cream parlor
Opened store on weekends and handled some bookkeeping.

June to August 2004
Cashier (part-time)
Candy's Kitchen—restaurant
Operated cash register and counted money at the end of my shift.

REFERENCES

Available upon request.

Geoffery E. Pace

121 Corinne Avenue • Gary, IN 46408 • (218) 555-5452 • geofferypace@xxx.com

Immediate Objective

To gain a part-time position working in a local or state park. I seek
a position that will enable me to attend the local community college
and obtain an Associate's degree in Ranger Services.

Career Objective

To become a park ranger.

Previous Work Experience

6 / 04 - 8 / 04
Camp Carloads
1956 Vista Drive
Gary, IN 46408
Dishwasher

1 / 04 - 5 / 04
Gary Radio
92 Hanger Way
Gary, IN 46408
Phone solicitor

8 / 02 - 10 / 03
Burger King Restaurant
1782 Freedom Drive
Gary, IN 46408
Counter worker

Education

Gary High School, 2004
Gary, IN
GPA 2.7 / 4.0

School Activities

Member of the Sierra Club, 2004
Member of the jazz choir, 2002 - 2004
Member of the basketball team, 2003 - 2004

Additional Comments

I have also done yard work, including pulling weeds, splitting and stacking wood,
hauling brush, and cutting trees into manageable lengths. I especially enjoy
being outdoors. I learn quickly and have a well-developed work ethic.

Personal References

Available upon request.

LAURA T. MENDEZ
445 El Cerro Drive
Phoenix, AZ 85076
(602) 555-0739
laura.mendez@xxx.com

OBJECTIVE

To work for an executive who needs a full-time assistant to handle routine tasks and detail work.

WORK EXPERIENCE

10-03 to present
Fantasy Cakes, Phoenix, AZ
Position: Counterperson
Duties: Wait on customers, operate the cash register, take cake orders, and clean.

7-02 to 10-03
Mickey's One Hour Photo, Phoenix, AZ
Position: Counterperson
Duties: Wait on customers, operate the cash register, develop negatives, and print pictures.

7-01 to 6-02
Pioneer Museum, Phoenix, AZ
Position: Generalist
Duties: Type manuscripts, lead tours, and mow lawns.

OTHER EXPERIENCE

• President of high-school student council.
• Basketball coach for junior high.
• Member of 4-H horse club.

EDUCATION

Murray High School—2004
GPA 3.57/4.00

RELEVANT COURSE WORK

Keyboarding	one year—64 wpm
Accounting	one semester
Computer Literacy	one semester
Word Processing	one year

REFERENCES

Will be available upon request.

MARIA G. FORTUNE

571 Vienna Drive • Pikeville, KY 41501

(606) 555-5941 • MariaFortune@xxx.net

OBJECTIVE
To obtain an entry-level job in business with the opportunity to advance to management.

EDUCATION
I am a 2004 graduate of Pikeville High School.
My grade point average was 3.85/4.00.

I have taken courses in Accounting, Word Processing, and Keyboarding (50 wpm).
I can use both IBM-compatible and Macintosh computers.

WORK EXPERIENCE
May 2002–February 2003
Dick Bruhns
Pikeville, KY
Responsibilities:
Assisted customers with purchases and operated cash register.

August 2001–May 2002
Jacob's Drugstore
Pikeville, KY
Responsibilities:
Wrapped customers' purchases, assisted customers, and operated cash register.

May–August 2001
Fischer Corporation
Pikeville, KY
Responsibilities:
Worked on inventory and did light bookkeeping.

EXTRACURRICULAR ACTIVITIES
• Member of student government, 2002, 2004.
• Member of yearbook staff, 2003, 2004.
• Member of volleyball team, 2001–2004.

REFERENCES
Available upon request.

ADAM E. QUAN

571 Miller Court • Slidell, LA 70460 • (504) 555-1809 • adamquan@xxx.com

OBJECTIVE

To use my organizational and analytical skills in the financial industry while I continue my education toward a career as a Certified Public Accountant.

EDUCATION

Slidell High School, 2004
I plan to attend Grambling State University in Grambling, LA, and receive my Bachelor's degree in Accounting in 2008.

EMPLOYMENT

November 2003 to June 2004
Dave's Deli Restaurant, Slidell, LA
• Managed cash receipts and cash flow of customers' activity as a cashier.
• Maintained good customer relations through hosting.
• Provided clean work areas by bussing workstations.

June 2003 to September 2003
The Lodge, Slidell, LA
• Handled the opening and closing procedures of both the restaurant and store facility.
• Responsible for customer service, which included cashiering, bussing workstations, and hosting.

November 2001 to June 2002
Dave's Deli Restaurant, Slidell, LA
• Trained as a cashier; learned how to manage cash transactions.
• Handled payment transactions for customers.
• Trained in the importance of customer relations through hosting.

REFERENCES AVAILABLE UPON REQUEST.

PABLO A. RAMIREZ

261 Baltusrol Way
Baton Rouge, LA 70803
(504) 555-5069
pablo_ramirez@xxx.com

JOB GOAL
A permanent part-time position as a salesperson and cashier

EDUCATION
Central High School, 2005
143 Central Street, Baton Rouge, LA 70803
Course work for a Business major:
- Accounting
- Economics
- Psychology

SCHOOL ACTIVITIES
- Four-year member of football team
- Four-year member of SADD (Students Against Drunk Driving)
- Three-year member of the Business Club; President my final year

WORK EXPERIENCE
Blockbuster Video
435 Desilva Street
Baton Rouge, LA 70803
Duties: sales and cashiering

Sidney's Food Store
200 Desilva Street
Baton Rouge, LA 70803
Duties: sales, cashiering, and answering the telephone

PERSONAL STATEMENT
I am a warm, sincere person who is eager to learn and willing to work hard.

REFERENCES
Available upon request

JAMES C. RICHARDS
1740 Webster Woods Dr.
Lake Charles, LA 70609
(318) 555-2347
jamesrichards@xxx.com

Career Objective
A position in business management in which I can use my skills in the areas of strategic management, business research, and information management.

Education
Lake Charles High School Graduate, 2005
GPA 3.4 / 4.0

Relevant Courses
) Advanced Mathematics
) AP Computer Science
) Business I, II
) Accounting

Work History
Hughes Union 76
Lake Charles, LA
April 2003 to September 2005
Station Attendant
Duties: Helped customers at gas pumps. Did minor mechanical repairs: radiator hoses, tires, batteries, and belts. This job indicates my ability to work with demanding and frustrated customers in pressure situations.

Tribune (newspaper)
Lake Charles, LA
June 2002 to September 2002
Paper Inserter
Duties: Began work at 12:00 A.M. and prepared newspapers for delivery. The job was usually completed in four hours. This job indicates my ability to work diligently regardless of time of day.

References available upon request.

NICOLA E. RHODES
938 Indiana Avenue
Augusta, ME 04330
(207) 555-5809
NicolaRhodes@xxx.com

OBJECTIVE

To obtain a part-time position with a firm whose focus is public relations. The position should lead to full-time employment after graduation from college.

EDUCATION

2004, Student at Farmington University
Business and French major

2003, Graduate of Augusta High School
GPA 3.8/4.0

SPECIAL ABILITIES AND STUDIES

I have taken advanced courses in Mathematics, French, English Literature, Business, Science, and Computer Technology and Programming.

I speak fluent French.

I am experienced with a computerized cash register.

PREVIOUS EMPLOYMENT

Burger King Restaurant
200 Main Street, Augusta, ME
September 1999 to August 2003

Duties:
• Cashiering (computerized)
• Food preparation
• Dishwashing

REFERENCES AVAILABLE UPON REQUEST

Martha Bigelow
martha.bigelow@xxx.com

Current Address:
468 East 25th Street
Charlottesville, VA 22906
(804) 555-8723

Permanent Address:
2005 Bristol Avenue
Richmond, VA 23284
(804) 555-9737

OBJECTIVE

An entry-level systems analyst position for a manufacturing or software firm. Desire to progress to position providing systems management to client companies. Seek an opportunity to use my leadership and communication skills.

EDUCATION

UNIVERSITY OF VIRGINIA, Charlottesville, VA
Bachelor of Science: expected May 2005, Computer Information Systems
Major GPA: 3.5

STUDENT EXCHANGE PROGRAM, Florence, Italy: Summer 2002

RELEVANT EXPERIENCE

5/04–8/04
AT&T GLOBAL INFORMATION SOLUTIONS, Milan, Italy
Intern, Financial Planning and Inventory Accounting Departments: Analyzed improvements in time, money, and paperwork that would result from the use of the new purchasing system. Performed cost analysis of new PC units for future pricing. Wrote macros in Excel and Word to make exporting of files easier in each file format. Translated reports, letters, and phone calls from Italian to English and vice versa.

8/03–4/04
AT&T, Charlottesville, VA
Communications Representative: Marketed the AT&T MasterCard, phone card, and phone company to students.

5/03–8/03
RICHMOND HILLS TENNIS CLUB, Richmond, VA
Tennis Instructor: Developed and managed a tennis program for pupils of different ages and skill levels at a community facility. Marketed the program aggressively. Hired four tennis instructors because of program's growth.

ACTIVITIES

DELTA SIGMA PI BUSINESS FRATERNITY
Offices Held: Vice President for chapter operations, Secretary, Sergeant-at-Arms
Major Accomplishment: Launched first Mini Ironman Competition for American Cancer Society and raised more than $10,000.

UNIVERSITY OF VIRGINIA STUDENT GOVERNMENT
Governor: Elected to represent 500 students in Stern Hall.

ALPHA PHI SORORITY
Panhellenic Council Delegate: Served as a sorority liaison and representative.

UNIVERSITY OF VIRGINIA RECRUITING REPRESENTATIVE
Tour Guide: Led campus and dormitory tours for prospective university students.

PERSONAL INFORMATION

Skilled in Windows, C/C++, Perl, SQL, HTML, XML, PHP, Lotus, Excel, Word, and COBOL MVS. Traveled extensively in Europe. Fluent in Italian. Member of the Richmond High School State Champion Tennis Team. Enjoy tennis, jogging, and outdoor activities.

REFERENCES

Available on request.

CHRISTIANNA M. NELSON
900 Bear Valley Drive • Escanaba, MI 49829 • (906) 555-2380
C.Nelson@xxx.com

IMMEDIATE OBJECTIVE
To obtain a position as a physical therapist aide that enables me to work with physically disabled individuals while I attend college. I would prefer employment with a company that would be able to place me in a permanent physical therapist position once I have graduated from college.

LONG-TERM OBJECTIVE
To become a physical therapist.

EDUCATION
Escanaba High School in Escanaba, MI, 2004
GPA 3.9/4.0
My educational plans are to attend Calvin College in Grand Rapids, MI. I plan to major in Education of the Physically Handicapped.

ACADEMIC ACTIVITIES
I was a member of the high-school Interact Club (a community service organization) for four years. I was president of the club my senior year.

EMPLOYMENT HISTORY
Summers 2002, 2003
BAY DE NOC CAMP, Madison, WI
Camp Counselor for developmentally disabled teenagers and adults.

Academic years 2001, 2002, 2003
ESCANABA HIGH SCHOOL, Escanaba, MI
Volunteer Aide to Special Education teacher.

REFERENCES AVAILABLE UPON REQUEST.

Kyle J. Ahn

kyleahn@xxx.net
589 Bavington Drive
Nashville, TN 37209
(615) 555-4589

Objective

Full-time employment in the field of business management.

Work Experience

Kroger
Nashville, TN
Position: Courtesy Clerk
Responsibilities: Bagging groceries, serving customers, and maintaining site.
June to August 2004

The Fish Bowl Pet Center
Nashville, TN
Position: Assistant Manager
Responsibilities: Selling, maintaining shop, ordering supplies, closing out register, opening and closing the store.
June to August 2003

Special Skills

Proficient with Word and Excel
Keyboarding—60 wpm
Able to work well with customers and coworkers

Education

Graduate of Memorial High School—2004
GPA: 2.75/4.00
Four-year member of boys' volleyball team
Four-year member of Business Club
My future educational goals are to attend Nashville State Technical Institute part-time, majoring in Business. I plan to work full-time while attending college.

References

Peter Lane, owner, The Fish Bowl, (615) 555-0765, peter.lane@xxx.com
Donna Staley, neighbor, (615) 555-1365, d.staley@xxx.com
Ron Nix, family friend, (615) 555-5502, ronnix@xxx.com

◆ Joshua K. Peck ◆

301 Coates Drive • International Falls, MN 56649
(218) 555-2452 • jkpeck@xxx.com

◆ ◆ ◆

◆ Objective
To become a professional actor.

◆ Acting Experience
* Member of the Drama Club for four years.
* Major role in *The People vs Maxine Loe*, 2003.
* Major role in *Our Town*, 2002.
* Major role in *Arsenic and Old Lace*, 2001.

◆ Work Experience
June 2003 to Present
McDonald's Restaurant
International Falls, MN
Responsibilities: operate cash register, improve and maintain the site and lobby, make fries, cook the food, and close the restaurant at night.

June 2002 to August 2002
Taco Bell Restaurant
International Falls, MN
Responsibilities: operated electronic cash register, prepared and packaged the food, and cleaned and maintained the restaurant.

◆ Personal
* Competed in track and field for six years.
* I was a multievent winner and team captain my senior year.
* Member of the football team for two years.
* Fluent in written and conversational French.

◆ Education
Graduated from International Falls High School in 2003.
Drama Society award winner, 2003.
Plan to attend St. Cloud State University in St. Cloud, MN, in 2005. I will major in Speech/Communication/Theater Education and will graduate in 2009.

◆ References
Available upon request.

JOSEFINA Y. ALONZO

236 Quail Run
Denver, CO 80222
(303) 555-1498
Mobile: (303) 555-8877
josefina_alonzo@xxx.com

OBJECTIVE
To become a professional ski instructor.

WORK EXPERIENCE
Winters, 2002, 2003, 2004
Ski Lift Operator, Ski Instructor
Vista Ski Area, Denver, CO
Worked lifts, reported problems, and taught children and adults how to ski.

June 2003 to August 2003
Busperson, Food Preparer
The Wild Side Cafe, Denver, CO
Bussed tables, washed dishes, and prepared food for the next day.

OTHER EXPERIENCE
Member of Denver Ski Rescue Team, 2004
Member of high-school ski team, 2001 to 2004
Member of Denver Youth Group, 2002

EDUCATION
Roosevelt High School, graduated 2004
Denver, CO

REFERENCES
References will be furnished upon request.

Frank P. Reyes

988 El Sereno Ct.

Stratham, NH 03885

(603) 555-1798

F.Reyes@xxx.com

OBJECTIVE

To work as a part-time chef while I attend classes at New Hampshire Culinary Academy in Stratham, NH. The job should include the possibility of promotion and a full-time position after I graduate from the Academy.

EDUCATION

Stratham High School, Stratham, NH
General Studies Diploma, 2004
GPA 2.9/4.0
Relevant Course Work:

Restaurant--internship	two semesters
Nutrition	one semester
Food Chemistry	two semesters
English	four years
French	four years

WORK EXPERIENCE

June 2003 to August 2003
Food Service Worker
Rudolph's Restaurant
267 Lahai Roi St., Stratham, NH 03885
Responsibilities: Preparing food for the next day, operating the cash register, and grill chef.

June 2002 to August 2002
Food Service Worker
Dairy Queen
489 Cross St., Stratham, NH 03885
Responsibilities: Managing cash flow, acting as night manager occasionally, operating the cash register, cooking, and preparing food.

REFERENCES WILL BE MADE AVAILABLE UPON YOUR REQUEST.

Tom Nguyen
234 Kingsbury Drive, Auburn, NY 13021
(315) 555-6757
tom.nguyen@xxx.com

Objective
To secure part-time employment in the field of business management while I continue my education.

Education
Auburn High School, 2003
GPA: 3.8/4.0
In the fall, I will attend Canisius College in Buffalo, NY. I plan to major in Business Administration and Management. I will graduate in 2007.

Activities
- *Volunteer food server at Friday's Food Center for the homeless twice a month.*
- *Four-year member of the Auburn High School speech group, Junior Statesmen of America.*
- *Four-year member of the Auburn High School Varsity Football Team, team captain senior year.*

Work Experience
June to August, 2001, 2002, 2003
Salesperson, Delivery Driver, Cashier
The One Stop Shop, Auburn, NY
I started in merchandising, became a cashier, and was promoted to delivery driver.

> *Special Skills: Built and sold furniture; designed and constructed promotional signs and merchandise displays; learned the workings of shipping and receiving departments; trained personnel for all jobs mentioned above.*

General
I am a creative worker who is artistically inclined. I can do challenging jobs thoroughly and efficiently. I am communicative with the public as well as with my fellow employees. I am capable of sticking with a job as is shown by my work experience.

References
Available when requested.

KIMBERLY C. BAKER

456 Baltusrol Way
Tarboro, NC 27886
(919) 555-0922
kimberly-baker@xxx.com

OBJECTIVE

A part-time job as a receptionist for a company that offers the possibility of promotion into business management.

EDUCATION

Tarboro High School, 2003
GPA 3.20/4.00
My educational plans are to attend Edgecombe Community College in Tarboro, NC, full-time for the next two years. I will transfer to East Carolina University in Greenville, NC, to obtain my Bachelor's degree in Business Administration and Management.

EXPERIENCE

RECEPTIONIST

Leon T. Beacom, CPA
Tarboro, NC
Summers 2002 and 2003
Responsibilities: Answering phones, taking messages, filing papers, and making client appointments.

SCOREKEEPER

Tarboro Youth Basketball Association
Tarboro, NC
November to February, 2001, 2002, and 2003
Responsibilities: Writing score sheets, recording the score, and reporting score results to the newspaper.

OTHER EXPERIENCE

- Member of Student Government at Tarboro High for three years. Associated Student Body President senior year.
- Member of the Tarboro High varsity basketball team for three years. Played junior varsity basketball for one year.
- Member of the Tarboro High varsity softball team for three years.
- Member of Tarboro High varsity track team for one year.
- Worked at the Special Olympics for two years.

REFERENCES UPON REQUEST

TRACEY WARRICK

467 Altivo Drive
Yellow Springs, OH 45387
(513) 555-1875
tracey.warrick@xxx.com

OBJECTIVE

To serve as a part-time travel agent in a firm that provides the possibility of advancement and a full-time position once I have graduated from college.

WORK EXPERIENCE

June 2004 to present
Word Processor, Data Entry
The Book Worm, Yellow Springs, OH
Responsibilities: Answering correspondence, entering data including accounts receivable, and mailing information.

Prior to June 2004
Miscellaneous jobs such as babysitting, house-sitting, and housecleaning.

OTHER EXPERIENCE

- Competitive Swimming: My participation with the Yellow Springs High School swim team and the Aqua Devils swim team has increased my ability to handle competition and stress.
- Leadership: I was in charge of the operation of the Yellow Springs High School Blood Bank for two years.
- Travel: I am experienced in many different kinds of travel, including camping, backpacking, and canoeing.

EDUCATION

June 2004 Graduate of Yellow Springs High School
GPA 2.6/4.0

I am currently enrolled in two night courses focused on the travel agency business: Regional Occupational Program and a computer course on the Apollo series working with the computerized OAG.

My educational plans are to major in Communications and to graduate from Antioch College in Yellow Springs, OH, in 2008.

References available upon request.

MATT M. LEROY
mleroy@xxx.com

College Address: Home Address:
45 East Campus Drive   33 Pleasant Drive
Ames, IA 50011   Storm Lake, IA 50588
(515) 555-9600   (712) 555-9232

OBJECTIVE
To obtain an entry-level position that uses my computer and business skills and challenges me to grow professionally.

EDUCATION
Iowa State University of Science and Technology, Ames, IA
Major: Applied Computer Science
Minor: Business Administration
Expected date of graduation: May 2005

RELEVANT COURSE WORK
Computer Application and Design, External Data Structures, Data Structures, Introduction to Systems Development, Database Processing, System Development Tools and Issues

WORK EXPERIENCE
5/04 to 8/04
Computer Programmer/Analyst Internship, Caterpillar, Inc., Des Moines, IA
Maintaining and testing online programs
Designing and testing batch programs using COBOL MVS

9/03 to 3/04
Maintenance Worker, Central Iowa Trucking, Storm Lake, IA
Keeping shop area in order, running errands
Computer data entry

1/02 to 8/03
Farm Worker, Peterson Farms, Storm Lake, IA
Year-round operation and maintenance of farm machinery

SKILLS
Able to use computers to solve problems
Fluent in COBOL MVS, C/C++, and Visual Basic
Experience with WordPerfect and Microsoft Office 2000

HONORS AND SCHOLARSHIPS
Iowa State University of Science and Technology Governor's Scholar, 2004
Freshman Entrance Writing Examination—winner
Iowa State Scholar, 2001
Storm Lake High School Valedictorian

ACTIVITIES
Varsity member of the university football and wrestling teams for four years

REFERENCES
Available upon request

DEBBIE R. NEWELL

2986 Middle Avenue
Rapid City, SD 57701
(605) 555-1307
debbienewell@xxx.com

OBJECTIVE
Full-time employment as a secretary while I attend night classes.

PARTICULARS
Typing: 75 wpm
WordPerfect, Word, Excel, PageMaker, Lotus, PowerPoint, Quicken

EDUCATION
Rapid City High School, Rapid City, SD
Degree: 2004, General Studies

I will attend Western Dakota Vocational Technical Institute for two years
beginning in the fall of 2005.

WORK EXPERIENCE
Kmart
Clerk, women's clothing department
Cash Register Operator
9/03 to present
Full-time during the summer
Part-time during the academic year

EXTRACURRICULAR
Member of the high-school choir and jazz choir.
Participated in Girl Scout activities for three years.
Served as a camp counselor for Brownies and Pixies at the City Park.

REFERENCES
Available upon your request.

CAROL M. LOOMIS

85 Peace Dr.
Portland, OR 97219
(503) 555-0186
carol.loomis@xxx.com

OBJECTIVE

A part-time position as a children's dance instructor that
will enable me to teach while attending college classes.

EDUCATION

June 2004 Graduate of Lakeside High School
Portland, OR
GPA 3.00/4.00
In Fall 2005, I will attend Lewis and Clark College in Portland, OR.
I will graduate in 2009 with a Bachelor's degree in Dramatic Arts.

WORK EXPERIENCE

Assistant Dance Instructor
The Dance Studio, Portland, OR
Responsibilities: teaching tap and jazz to school-aged children.
Summers 2002, 2003

SPECIAL ACTIVITIES

Two-year member of Jazz Dancers group in high school.
Four years of jazzercise.
Six years of tap and ballet lessons.

REFERENCES

Cathy Delude, dance instructor
The Dance Studio
(503) 555-1154
cathy.delude@xxx.com

Norman Haney, family friend
(503) 555-7600
nhaney@xxx.net

Norman L. Potter

4322 Clares Street
Butler, PA 16003
(412) 555-6897
Cell: (412) 555-6665
normanpotter@xxx.com

Objective

To obtain a part-time position with an architectural firm that will enable me to gain experience in the field of architecture. The position should provide the possibility for advancement with the completion of my scholastic studies.

Education

Butler High School, Butler, PA, 2005
Graduated in the top 20 percent of the class
GPA: 3.2/4.0
> Next year, I will attend Butler County Community College, where I plan to major in Drafting.

Relevant Skills

Completion of Drafting 1 and 2 courses in high school.
Proficient in Computer-Assisted Design.

Work Experience

Food Service Worker
June 2003 to August 2005
McDonald's Restaurant, Butler, PA
> Responsible for taking and filling food orders, operating the cash register, preparing food, cleaning lobby and food area, and stocking supplies.

General Worker
Prior to June 2003
Miscellaneous Jobs
> Performed babysitting and gardening tasks.

References available upon request.

MORGAN A. WRIGHT

896 Mesa Dr. • Columbia, SC 29208
(803) 555-4079 • m.a.wright@xxx.com

OBJECTIVE
To become a limousine driver

WORK EXPERIENCE
Columbia Pizza Company, Columbia, SC
Dough Roller
Responsibilities:
• Providing a clean work area
• Flouring the table
• Rolling and cutting the dough
• Mixing the dough batch for the following day

The Supreme Pizza, Columbia, SC
Busperson
Responsibilities:
• Completing "prep list"
• Collecting dishes
• Putting dishes away
• Cleaning restaurant and closing up

OTHER EXPERIENCE
Hold South Carolina chauffeur's license
Member of DeYoung High School Jazz Band

EDUCATION
Recent graduate of DeYoung High School
Columbia, SC

Full references will be provided on request.

AMY J. FENNELL

445 Polo Drive
Portland, OR 97201
(503) 555-1967
amyfennell@xxx.com

OBJECTIVE

To be a fashion designer.

EDUCATION

High School: Upland High School
Degree: High-school diploma, 2005
Grade Average: B
In the fall of 2005, I will attend Bassist College in Portland, OR, where
I plan to receive an Associate's degree in fashion design.

ACTIVITIES

During my junior year I helped start a new group at Upland High School
called SDI (the Student Design Initiative). I was the group's treasurer my
senior year.

I was a member of Junior Statesmen of America (JSA) my junior and
senior years.

My sophomore and junior years, I kept statistics for the junior varsity
basketball team.

During my freshman year, I kept statistics for the freshman basketball
team.

WORK EXPERIENCE

Miscellaneous jobs such as lawn mowing and babysitting.

References will be provided upon your request.

Johnny K. Litchfield

452 Baja Sol Drive
Sioux Falls, SD 57197
(605) 555-9506
johnny.litchfield@xxx.com

Objective	A permanent position as a carpenter
Work Experience	Jack's Pizza Sioux Falls, SD Dishwasher Period of Service: four months
Education	2003 Graduate of Sioux Falls High School Grade Average B- Relevant Courses: Construction I, II Mechanical Drawing
Special Skills	Woodworking Three years as a hobby Landscaping One year in home garden Bassist Currently performing in a band
References	Jack Core Owner, Jack's Pizza (605) 555-0793 jackcore@xxx.net Richard Crivello Family Friend (605) 555-3702 RichardCrivello@xxx.com

ANGELA R. CHACON

564 Meadowview Court
Castleton, VT 05735
(802) 555-8102
angela.chacon@xxx.com

OBJECTIVE
To work in the art/graphic design department of an advertising agency.

WORK EXPERIENCE
Customer Relations/Secretary
Designs Unlimited
Castleton, VT
June to August 2004

Office Assistant
Penn Ad Agency
Castleton, VT
June to August 2003

Babysitting
Prior to June 2003

OTHER EXPERIENCE
Member of yearbook staff, 2003 to 2004
Member of Castleton Scholarship Federation, 2003 to 2004
Member of varsity tennis and softball teams, 2002 to 2004
Fluent in Spanish

EDUCATION
I graduated from Castleton High School in June 2004. My educational plans are to attend Castleton State College in Castleton, VT, where I will major in Drawing and Fine Arts.

REFERENCES
Will be provided upon your request.

NAME	Carla Grant
ADDRESS	2976 Lucky Lane Cleveland, TN 37320
TELEPHONE	(615) 555-1745
E-MAIL	carlagrant@xxx.net
OBJECTIVE	Full-time position in a clothing store as a salesclerk.
EDUCATION	Knoxville High School, 2004 Knoxville, TN GPA 3.0/4.0 My educational plans are to attend Cleveland State Community College part-time. I will major in Marketing and Sales.
EXPERIENCE	JCPenney May 2004 to present Cash register operator The Emporium January 1998 to November 2003 Salesclerk
EXTRACURRICULAR	Junior Achievement, 2003, 2004 Member of Zenith Group (a public speaking club), 2004 Sophomore Magazine Sales -- Class Coordinator, 2002
QUALIFICATIONS	I am a committed, hardworking, and punctual employee who interacts skillfully with customers.
REFERENCES	Kay Dietze, Junior Achievement Sponsor (615) 555-2778, kaydietze@xxx.com Linda Nealis, JCPenney (615) 555-4410, lnealis@xxx.com

RENALDO G. MADRIGAL

290 Hampshire Rd. • Provo, UT 84602 • (901) 555-1834
renaldo_madrigal@xxx.com

OBJECTIVE
Part-time managerial position with a small business.

WORK EXPERIENCE
June 2004 to present
Arco Station
Provo, UT
Station Attendant
Responsibilities: Operating cash register, light stocking, and cleaning.

March 2004 to June 2004
The Water Hole
Provo, UT
Swim School Maintenance
Responsibilities: Added chlorine to pool as necessary and cleaned and
vacuumed pool.

Prior to March 2004
Woodland Timber
Woodcutter and Splitter
Responsibilities: Cut, split, and hauled wood for personal use and profit.

OTHER EXPERIENCE
• Experienced in fiberglass repair.
• Member of Utah Scholarship Federation--four years.
• Member of varsity soccer team--two years. Team captain senior year.
• Member of junior varsity soccer team. Received valuable player award--
  2002.
• Fluent in Spanish.
• Member of Big Brother, Big Sister program--three years.

EDUCATION
2004 Graduate of Provo High School
GPA 3.1/4.0
• My educational plans are to attend Brigham Young University in Provo,
  UT. My degree objective is to obtain a B.A. in Business.

References will be provided upon your request.

• DALE CRIVELLO

275 Huntington Drive
Middlebury, VT 05753
(802) 555-4294
dalecrivello@xxx.com

• OBJECTIVE

Part-time position as a chef or assistant chef providing the opportunity of advancement upon my graduation from college.

• EDUCATION

Middlebury High School
2004 graduate
GPA: 3.5/4.0
Relevant course work:
• Mathematics through Geometry
• Home Economics 1 and 2
• Nutrition
• Two years of French

I will attend New England Culinary Institute in Montpelier, VT, in the fall. I will major in Food Production, Management, and Services.

• WORK EXPERIENCE

2/03–8/03
Denny's Restaurant
    I was the preparation cook.

6/02–8/02
Swensen's Ice Cream Factory
    I dipped cones and decorated various ice-cream products.

• OTHER EXPERIENCE

• Varsity football team, four years, MVP senior year
• Soccer league, four years
• Ski club, four years

• REFERENCES

Available on request.

ROGER NEWTON
765 Murphy's Lane
Arlington, VA 22207
(703) 555-3099
rogernewton@xxx.com

OBJECTIVE
To become a full-time auto mechanic

EDUCATION
2004 graduate of Arlington High School
Relevant course work:

Auto Shop	two years
Auto Shop student supervisor	one year
Business Math	one year

EXPERIENCE
6/04 to present
ARLINGTON SHELL, Arlington, VA
Station Attendant
Responsible for operating cash register, assisting customers, checking oil, washing windows, checking tire pressure, and fixing flat tires

Prior to 6/04
ODD JOBS
Gardening, dog walking, catering, cleanup work, and car repair

ACTIVITIES
Four-year member high-school morning weight-lifting club
Two-year member high-school spirit club
One-year member high-school business club

INTERESTS
Customizing vans
Attending NASCAR races
Racing motorcycles

REFERENCES PROVIDED ON REQUEST

ANTOINETTE JACKSON

5071 Illinois Rd. • Santa Fe, NM 87504

(505) 555-5452 • a-jackson@xxx.com

GOAL

A part-time position as a receptionist.

EDUCATION

9 / 01 to present

College of Santa Fe, anticipate Bachelor's degree in Theological Studies
(with Honors), June 2005.

Current GPA: 3.7 / 4.0

EXPERIENCE

2001 to present

Tutor, College of Santa Fe Christian Ministries Tutoring Program.

Volunteer on a weekly basis with an underprivileged child.

2000 to present

Youth Fellowship, Santa Fe Presbyterian Church.

Lead small group Bible studies. Coordinate welcoming and hospitality committees. Participate in prayer groups. Serve at soup kitchens.

7 / 04 to 9 / 04

Counselor, Hill Top Lodge, Albuquerque, NM.

Led Bible studies. Taught athletics and lifestyle seminars for high school students.

10 / 03 to 12 / 03

Security Agent, College of Santa Fe Bookstore.

Handled surveillance activities and arrest of violators. Also, ensured store safety and transported funds.

6 / 00 to 9 / 02

Services Department, Osee, Ling (law firm), Santa Fe, NM.

Dealt with court filings, couriers, faxes, mail, and distribution. Acted as receptionist.

ADDITIONAL INFORMATION

* Participated with my high-school youth group on several work projects at churches and orphanages in Mexico.
* Treasurer, Chi Omega House, College of Santa Fe.
* Social Chairman, Freshman Orientation Committee, College of Santa Fe.

References available upon request.

JASMINE K. LAKE
jklake@xxx.com

Present Address:
P.O. Box 04834
Baltimore, MD 21218
(301) 555-0523

Permanent Address:
5606 Castle Avenue
Langston, OK 73050
(405) 555-3247

OBJECTIVE

To obtain a position in the entering class of a top medical school and pursue a career in research-oriented medicine.

EDUCATION

Johns Hopkins University, Baltimore, MD
Bachelor of Science, Biology, with honors, June 2004
Overall GPA: 3.83
Science GPA: 3.89

RESEARCH EXPERIENCE

Research Investigator, Molecular Endocrinology Lab, Johns Hopkins Medical Center (2002–2004).

Studied the relationship between stem-cell factor protein and the Sertoli cell and germ cell arrest male infertility syndromes. Assisted on projects studying inhibin protein transcription and translation rates. Helped plan, coordinate, and carry out research. Learned and used techniques such as Southern blots, cell cultures, reverse transcriptase polymerase chain reactions, and single-stranded conformational polymorphism. Prepared data and reports for publication.

Research and Clinical Assistant, Department of Neurology, Baltimore Veteran's Administration Outpatient Clinic (2001).

Studied neuromuscular diseases and the ability of human muscle to survive different methods of storage. Learned a variety of pathology techniques. Assisted with neurological examinations such as EEGs.

OTHER WORK EXPERIENCE

Tutor, Johns Hopkins University, Baltimore, MD (2001–2002).
Assisted other students with English, Mathematics, Physics, and Biology.

ADDITIONAL INFORMATION

- Member, Student Radio Board of Directors, Johns Hopkins University.
- Volunteer, "Tiny Tots" Nursery School, Johns Hopkins Special
  Olympics, Drunk Driving Prevention Program, and Free Peer Tutoring.
- Member, Committee on Housing and Residential Education, Johns
  Hopkins University.

REFERENCES

Available upon your request.

Stephanie Brown

stephanie.brown@xxx.com

Present Address:
P.O. Box 5041
Baton Rouge, LA 70802
(504) 555-2398

Permanent Address:
7893 Virginian Lane
Ashland, KY 41101
(606) 555-1365

Objective

To secure a part-time design consultant position with the possibility to work full-time upon my graduation

Education

Grantham College of Engineering
9/01 to present
Expect to graduate in 12/05 with Bachelor's degree in Computer Engineering

Experience

Summer Intern
6/04–9/04
Tandem Computers, Slidell, LA
• Worked with Mechanical Design Group
• Managed the receiving and shipping of prototype parts
• Assembled and evaluated prototype parts and systems
• Redesigned problem parts
• Edited and prepared graphic design for departmental handbook

Part-Time Intern
6/03–9/03
Pillar Corporation, Ashland, KY
• Learned the inside workings of a small design consulting firm
• Researched current products to focus design of new concepts
• Designed ideas for new dinnerware sets

Summer Intern
6/02–9/02
Praxis Design, Inc., Ashland, KY
• Used visual editors to alter program resources
• Edited program code
• Designed program icons and screens

Current Activities

Member, Kappa Kappa Gamma Sorority

References

Available upon request

Chapter 6

Sample Cover Letters

This chapter contains sample cover letters for students and graduates who are pursuing a wide variety of jobs and careers.

There are many different styles of cover letters in terms of layout, level of formality, and presentation of information. These samples also represent people with varying amounts of education and work experience. Choose one cover letter or borrow elements from several different cover letters to help you construct your own.

Martha Bigelow
martha.bigelow@xxx.com

Current Address:
468 East 25th Street
Charlottesville, VA 22906
(804) 555-8723

Permanent Address:
2005 Bristol Avenue
Richmond, VA 23284
(804) 555-9737

March 5, 2005

William Benedict
Federated Phone Company
87 Commercial Street
Santa Clara, CA 95054

Dear Mr. Benedict:

Dick Poon of AT&T referred me to you because of your firm's need for an analyst to evaluate the costs and pricing of several of your new communications products. I would be very interested in discussing this position with you.

I will be graduating from the University of Virginia in May 2005. My studies at the university have prepared me well to contribute to your organization. My quantitative skills have been sharpened by course work in Calculus and Statistics.

At AT&T, I received firsthand exposure to the pricing of new PC units. I believe that the tools I acquired there could effectively be translated to analyzing your company's products.

My resume is enclosed for your review. I will call you on Friday to set up an appointment to talk about how I might be useful to Federated Phone Company. I look forward to meeting with you.

Sincerely,

Martha Bigelow

Enclosure

Stephanie Brown

stephanie.brown@xxx.com

Present Address:
P.O. Box 5041
Baton Rouge, LA 70802
(504) 555-2398

Permanent Address:
7893 Virginian Lane
Ashland, KY 41101
(606) 555-1365

September 20, 2005

Knute Jameson
Entergy
Human Resources Department
225 Baronne Street
New Orleans, LA 70112

Dear Mr. Jameson:

This letter is in response to your advertisement in the *New Orleans Picayune* on September 18, 2005, for a design consultant.

Currently, I am pursuing my Bachelor's degree in Computer Engineering at Grantham College of Engineering. I plan to graduate in December 2005. I have taken several courses in Computer Programming as part of my major and feel confident of my ability to learn and master any design program.

Through my summer employment, I have gained practical experience in design concepts using computer programming. I believe that my work experience will allow me to make an immediate and valuable contribution to Entergy.

As requested, I am enclosing my resume for your review. I would appreciate the opportunity to discuss my qualifications and abilities in more depth at an interview.

Sincerely yours,

Stephanie Brown

enclosure

48 Hickory Drive
Houston, TX 77002
(713) 555-4968
heathermoreno@xxx.net

May 23, 2005

Joseph Lanz
Lanz and Associates at Law
2100 Main Street
Houston, TX 77002

Dear Mr. Lanz:

Thank you for talking with me on May 21, 2005, about the secretarial position at your law office. Our conversation made me very interested in becoming a member of your staff. With my past work experience and extensive course work in Accounting, Mathematics, and Keyboarding (56 wpm), I feel that I could be a valuable employee at Lanz and Associates at Law.

This June, I will graduate from Victoria High School. Should I be hired at your law firm, I would be available to work full-time from the 12th of June to the 24th of August. From August 24th on, I would be able to work a maximum of five hours each day. My work hours would be reduced because I will be attending college.

Thank you for your time. I look forward to hearing from you soon.

Sincerely,

Heather Moreno

ELLY G. MINCH

245 Chaparral Drive
Chester, NH 03036
(603) 555-1364
EMinch@xxx.com

August 9, 2005

Manchester Café
438 Third Street
Manchester, NH 03036

To Whom It May Concern:

I am writing in response to the Manchester Café's advertisement in the *New Hampshire Sunday News*. The position of part-time cashier greatly interests me as I have had similar jobs and enjoyed them.

In September, I will be a full-time student at Notre Dame College. I am seeking a position such as yours that will permit me to attend classes and partly finance my education.

The enclosed resume illustrates my past experience working as a cashier at two retail food establishments. I would be pleased if you contacted me for an interview at your earliest convenience. Thank you.

Sincerely,

Elly G. Minch

Enclosure

TRACEY WARRICK

467 Altivo Drive
Yellow Springs, OH 45387
(513) 555-1875
tracey.warrick@xxx.com

July 1, 2004

Ronald Wright
Travel Tours
354 High Street
Springfield, OH 45501

Dear Mr. Wright:

Please accept this letter as my application for the travel agent position available at your firm.

I have just received my diploma from Yellow Springs High School and am eager to begin my career in the travel industry. Presently, I am enrolled in a Regional Occupational Program travel course and a computer course on the Apollo series. Furthermore, my current employment has enabled me to become an excellent word processor and given me experience in handling correspondence.

I feel that my educational and professional background represent the qualifications you are seeking for this position. I look forward to setting a date for an interview during which we can discuss the position and share our expectations.

Thank you in advance for your consideration.

Sincerely,

Tracey Warrick

MARVIN HOPKINS

marvinhopkins@xxx.com
341 Beach Pines Drive
Olympia, WA 98505
(206) 555-2397

July 28, 2005

Charlene Butterfield
Human Resources Office
Computech
11156 Broadway
Redmond, WA 98052

Dear Ms. Butterfield:

I have been extremely impressed by your firm's successful entrance into the highly competitive personal computer marketplace. The young and aggressive nature of Computech appeals to me.

As a recent graduate of Eastern Washington University in Computer and Information Sciences, I am looking for a permanent position as a project engineer. Ideally, my employment would offer the possibility for advancement to a management position in research and development.

I worked with Microsoft during my summer vacations in 2003 and 2004. During my employment, I was a member of a four-person team that installed and implemented a 60-node 3Com 3Plus local area network. I have also provided both hardware and software support for Windows-compatible personal computers.

A resume is enclosed that reflects my academic, technical, and professional history. I am confident that my background in the computer industry would make me an asset to Computech.

I look forward to hearing from you soon. Thank you for your consideration.

Sincerely,

Marvin Hopkins

Douglas P. Shaw

191 Cuesta Way
Boise, ID 83706
(208) 555-8599
DPShaw@xxx.com

April 6, 2005

Eleanor Johnson
The Idaho Statesman
440 Lincoln Street
Boise, ID 83706

Dear Ms. Johnson:

I am writing to you with the hope that there is an opening for a photographer at your newspaper.

For four years, I have been a photographic assistant at Precious Moments Photography. I set up the lights and cameras, mix chemicals, develop film, and print photographs. I am also comfortable with many digital editing programs, including Adobe Photoshop and CorelDraw. As head photographer for my high school's yearbook, I took photographs of my classmates at sporting and social activities throughout the year. I have enclosed some of the photographs that were used in your newspaper's sports section.

I am hardworking, creative, and imaginative. I enjoy challenging work and perform well under pressure. I believe that these traits could be useful in highlighting news events for your newspaper.

I would appreciate the opportunity to meet with you to discuss any openings for photographers. I thank you for your consideration and look forward to hearing from you.

Sincerely,

Douglas P. Shaw

enclosures

MELISSA L. JUNG
1530 Hansen Lane
Dover, DE 19901
(302) 555-9401
melissa.jung@xxx.net

June 12, 2005

Mr. John Schwartz
Dover Unified School District
287 Central Avenue
Dover, DE 19901

Dear Mr. Schwartz:

I am writing to inquire whether the Dover Unified School District has an opening for an elementary school teacher. Having a Master's degree in Education and experience as an assistant art teacher in your district, I feel that I am well-qualified to be a teacher.

My personal experience as a mother of four children and as a hostess for six foreign exchange students has taught me how to relate effectively with young people. In addition, I have demonstrated my firm commitment to the community by leading the fund-raising efforts for the new elementary school and serving meals to homeless people at the soup kitchen.

I would appreciate the opportunity to discuss my qualifications and abilities with you at length in an interview.

Sincerely,

Melissa L. Jung

765 Murphy's Lane
Arlington, VA 22207
(703) 555-3099
rogernewton@xxx.com

May 15, 2005

Mr. Paul Evans, Manager
Arlington Motors Service Department
4900 Speedway
Arlington, VA 22207

Dear Mr. Evans:

I am interested in becoming an automotive mechanic for Arlington Motors. I also would like to participate in the automotive training program that your dealership sponsors.

While attending Arlington High School, I took all the automotive courses offered as well as Business Math. During the past year, I have been a station attendant at the Arlington Shell, where I have made minor repairs to customers' cars and helped the station's mechanics with major repairs. In my free time, I customize vans.

I would like to meet with you to discuss opportunities at Arlington Motors. I can be reached by telephone at (703) 555-3099. Thank you for your time.

Sincerely,

Roger Newton

BRIAN KANEKO
P.O. Box 4855
Stanford, CA 94309
(650) 555-1007
briankaneko@xxx.com

February 10, 2005

Judy Andrews
Mesa Engineering
3500 Camelback Drive
Phoenix, AZ 85032

Dear Ms. Andrews:

I would like to obtain an appointment with a representative of your firm to interview for the entry-level construction management position advertised at the Stanford University Placement Center.

My education and work experiences have prepared me to contribute to Mesa Engineering. I will receive my Master's degree in Civil Engineering from Stanford University in May. My course work has focused on Construction Management. In addition, my summer work experiences on projects have honed my technical and organizational skills.

A copy of my resume is enclosed for your evaluation. If you need further information, I will be pleased to provide you with the necessary materials.

I look forward to meeting with a representative of your firm to discuss my qualifications.

Sincerely,

Brian Kaneko

Enclosure

CHRISTIANNA M. NELSON
900 Bear Valley Drive • Escanaba, MI 49829 • (906) 555-2380
C.Nelson@xxx.com

July 1, 2004

Dr. Diane Wilson
ACME Physical Therapy and Sports Rehabilitation Clinic
489 South First Avenue
Grand Rapids, MI 49505

Dear Dr. Wilson:

I am writing concerning possible employment opportunities with your clinic. In particular, I am looking for a position as an assistant physical therapist that would permit me to work with physically disabled individuals while I attend college.

In September, I will start studies at Calvin College where I plan to major in Education of the Physically Handicapped. I would be available for part-time work at that time.

I have had direct experience in dealing with physically disabled people. At Bay de Noc Camp, I was camp counselor for developmentally disabled teenagers and adults, and at Escanaba High School, I assisted the Special Education teacher.

I would be delighted to meet with you at your convenience to discuss opportunities at your clinic.

Sincerely,

Christianna M. Nelson

• DALE CRIVELLO

275 Huntington Drive
Middlebury, VT 05753
(802) 555-4294
dalecrivello@xxx.com

August 9, 2004

Manager
Covington Inn
300 Main Street
Montpelier, VT 05602

Dear Manager:

I am writing in response to your advertisement in the August 8, 2004, issue of the *Times Argus*. I would appreciate the opportunity to talk to you about your inn's need for a preparation cook.

In Middlebury, I was the preparation cook for Denny's Restaurant. I was responsible for making all salads, including Chef's, Caesar, and Shrimp Louis. This fall I will be attending the New England Culinary Institute in your city where I plan to major in Food Production, Management, and Services. I am confident that my past experience and present training would be of benefit to your inn's restaurant.

I have enclosed my resume for your consideration. I hope to have a chance to speak with you about the position.

Yours truly,

Dale Crivello

enclosure

ELIZABETH M. LEIGH-WOOD
387 Sunny Hills Drive
Madison, WI 53711
(608) 555-1524
e.leigh-wood@xxx.net

April 24, 2004

Ms. Lorraine Sorenson
Madison Community Recreation Center
1500 Third Avenue SE
Madison, WI 53711

Dear Ms. Sorenson:

I am writing to follow up on our April 23rd telephone conversation about the lifeguard position. As we discussed, I have been certified in Standard First Aid and CPR. Furthermore, I was a lifeguard for Sunny Hills Neighborhood Club pool during the summer of 2002.

If I meet your requirements, I would be available for employment from June 1st to August 15th when I will begin my freshman year at Cardinal Stritch University.

My resume is enclosed as you requested. I look forward to hearing from you soon.

Sincerely,

Elizabeth M. Leigh-Wood

enclosure

JOHN NOWARK
john.nowark@xxx.com
217 Arthur Avenue
Omaha, NE 68103
(402) 555-5003

July 30, 2005

Bob Perkins, Superintendent
Sunburst Golf Course
One Sunburst Way
Lincoln, NE 68502

Dear Mr. Perkins:

I wish to apply for the position of assistant greenkeeper. John Niles of Oak Brook Golf Course told me about this opening and suggested that I contact you.

Currently, I am a nursery assistant at Sugar Hill Nursery in Omaha. In this position, I have become familiar with the care of many varieties of grasses, trees, plants, and shrubs. Also, I took Horticulture and Biology courses in high school. I am self-motivated and work well independently.

I will call you next week to follow up on this letter. Thank you in advance for your consideration.

Sincerely,

John Nowark

CRAIG L. HJORRING

31 Anderson Road • Fort Collins, CO 80523
(303) 555-0469 • craig.hjorring@xxx.com

February 10, 2005

Mr. Michael Chambers
Sports First
1874 Mountain Boulevard
Denver, CO 80203

Dear Mr. Chambers:

I would be very interested in talking with you about a marketing career at
Sports First.

Presently, I am pursuing a Bachelor's degree in Business Administration and
Management with an emphasis in Marketing. I plan to graduate in May 2005.

During the past three summers, I have worked at Sutherland Sports Wear.
I started as a sales representative and was promoted to assistant regional sales
manager. The following are a few of my accomplishments at Sutherland Sports
Wear that may interest your organization:

- Decreased advertising costs to 2.4 percent of sales.
- Increased sales by more than 20 percent each summer.
- Made industry contacts for joint venture opportunities.

I feel that my qualifications would enable me to be a productive member of
your marketing team.

Enclosed is my resume for your review. I look forward to meeting with you to
discuss employment opportunities at Sports First.

Sincerely,

Craig L. Hjorring

Enclosure

NICOLE ANNE CHANG

3089 McGlenn Drive • Jonesboro, AR 72402
(501) 555-9268 • nicole.chang@xxx.net

July 17, 2004

Dr. Melinda Cross
Cross Veterinary Hospital
378 Graham Road
Little Rock, AR 72202

Dear Dr. Cross:

I am interested in applying for employment as a manager at your veterinary hospital.

Recently, I graduated from Arkansas State University with a degree in Biology. I also have six months of experience working as a veterinary assistant. My duties included the administration of medicine and pacification of animals. I believe that my education and work experience would enable me to be a valuable asset to your hospital.

I would like to meet with you and demonstrate that I have the qualifications and the personality needed to make a successful hospital manager. I can be contacted at the above telephone number. Many thanks for your consideration.

Sincerely,

Nicole Anne Chang

JOSEPHINE ELIZABETH CROCKER
P.O. Box 317A • Trenton, NJ 08625
(609) 555-4832 • josephinecrocker@xxx.com

March 22, 2005

Ms. Louisa Brown, Director
Human Resources
New Jersey Health Department
P.O. Box 3000
Trenton, NJ 08625

Dear Ms. Brown:

This letter is in response to your advertisement for an environmental health inspector that appeared in the *Trentonian* on March 19, 2005. Please accept my resume in consideration for this position.

With a degree from Trenton State College in Environmental Health Science and two internships with county health departments in the environmental division, I believe that I am well suited to the state's health department needs.

Thank you for your time. I look forward to hearing from you soon regarding this position.

Sincerely,

Josephine E. Crocker

Sandra Singh
502 Sleigh Street
Stockton, CA 95211
(209) 555-2416
sandrasingh@xxx.com

January 11, 2005

Mr. Oliver Ford, Vice President
International Bank of New York
500 Broad Street
New York, NY 10050

Dear Mr. Ford:

I am writing to obtain further information regarding employment with your organization as a financial analyst. I strongly believe that international banking is an area in which my academic training, skill with languages and computers, and personal qualities would be an asset.

At the University of the Pacific, I am majoring in Political Science while also pursuing a Business focus. Course work in Accounting, Statistics, and Management has allowed me to develop the skills that are necessary to successfully perform financial analyses. Moreover, my past work experiences have provided me with opportunities to use and refine those skills in a business setting.

I appreciate your time and consideration. I hope to have the opportunity to talk with you in the near future.

Sincerely,

Sandra Singh

MATT M. LEROY
mleroy@xxx.com

College Address: Home Address:
45 East Campus Drive   33 Pleasant Drive
Ames, IA 50011   Storm Lake, IA 50588
(515) 555-9600   (712) 555-9232

April 28, 2005

Ms. Shari Fuller
Chicago Consultants Group
682 Market Street, Suite 10
Chicago, IL 60677

Dear Ms. Fuller:

I would greatly appreciate the opportunity to talk to you about your firm's need for a consultant analyst. I believe that my education at Iowa State University of Science and Technology in Applied Computer Science and Business Administration as well as my work at Caterpillar, Inc., would be useful to your computer consulting group.

Working at Chicago Consultants Group would be a unique and challenging experience. Your company has attracted me by its size and reputation in the field of consulting.

Enclosed is my resume. Thank you for your consideration.

Sincerely,

Matt M. LeRoy
enclosure